# A PARIS
# ALL YOUR OWN

ALSO BY ELEANOR BROWN

*The Weird Sisters*

*The Light of Paris*

# A PARIS
# ALL YOUR OWN

## BESTSELLING WOMEN WRITERS
## ON THE CITY OF LIGHT

*Edited by Eleanor Brown*

G. P. PUTNAM'S SONS

New York

PUTNAM

G. P. Putnam's Sons
*Publishers Since 1838*
An imprint of Penguin Random House LLC
375 Hudson Street
New York, New York 10014

*0'2|*

Copyright © 2017 by Eleanor Brown
Page 265 constitutes an extension of this copyright page

Library of Congress Cataloging-in-Publication Data

Names: Brown, Eleanor, [date] editor of compilation.
Title: A Paris all your own : bestselling women writers
on the City of Light / edited by Eleanor Brown.
Description: New York : G. P. Putnam's Sons, 2017. | Description based on
print version record and CIP data provided by publisher; resource not viewed.
Identifiers: LCCN 2017006748 (print) | LCCN 2017018615 (ebook) |
ISBN 9780399574481 (Ebook) | ISBN 9780399574474 (paperback)
Subjects: LCSH: Paris (France)—Description and travel. | Paris (France)—
Social life and customs. | Women authors—Travel—France—Paris. |
Paris (France)—Biography. | Women—France—Paris—Social life and customs. |
BISAC: LITERARY COLLECTIONS / Essays. | TRAVEL / Europe / France.
Classification: LCC DC707 (ebook) | LCC DC707 .P134 2017 (print) |
DDC 944/.361—dc23
LC record available at https://lccn.loc.gov/2017006748

Printed in the United States of America
3   5   7   9   10   8   6   4   2

Book design by Eve L. Kirch

To Chris Pepe,
with gratitude

# CONTENTS

Introduction      xi
*Eleanor Brown*

Thirteen Ways of Looking at a French Woman      1
*J. Courtney Sullivan*

Too Much Paris      18
*Michelle Gable*

Paris Is Your Mistress      41
*Ellen Sussman*

A Myth, a Museum, and a Man      51
*Susan Vreeland*

French for "Intrepid"      67
*Megan Crane*

Paris, Lost and Found      77
*Paula McLain*

Failing at Paris      88
*Eleanor Brown*

# CONTENTS

The Passion of Routine     105
    *Jennifer L. Scott*

Investigating Paris     114
    *Cara Black*

My Paris Dreams     128
    *M.J. Rose*

We'll Never Have Paris     147
    *Jennifer Coburn*

Reading Paris     169
    *Cathy Kelly*

Finding Paris's Hidden Past     182
    *Rachel Hore*

Secret Eatings     195
    *Julie Powell*

Until We Meet Again     208
    *Lauren Willig*

A Good Idea?     221
    *Therese Anne Fowler*

Paris Alone     231
    *Maggie Shipstead*

Thirty-Four Things You Should Know About Paris     247
    *Meg Waite Clayton*

Thanks to . . .     263

# INTRODUCTION

*Eleanor Brown*

What is it about Paris?

No other city's name conjures the same weight and cachet. To invoke Paris means something, makes whatever it touches more beautiful, more elegant, more . . . well, Parisian. Paris is berets and cafés, is romance and the lights on the Eiffel Tower, is wide boulevards and window boxes bright with flowers, is *Les Misérables* and Picasso and Chanel. Paris is so many things, all of them wonderful.

Its charm is one of the reasons Paris is one of the most-visited cities in the world, which is easy to believe if you've ever tried to catch a glimpse of the Mona Lisa at the Louvre on a summer Saturday. And Paris persists in literature as much as it does on postcards. There's a lengthy history of writers' obsession with the City of Light. There are innumerable books about it, from classics like *The Hunchback of Notre Dame* or *A Moveable Feast* or *Madeline* to cookbooks (including Ina Garten's *Barefoot in Paris*, which you should definitely not take literally) to the books written by the contributors in this collection.

I'd noticed the recent proliferation of Paris books, sure, from

Pamela Druckerman's *Bringing Up Bébé* to Paula McLain's block-buster *The Paris Wife*. I read them and loved them without connecting them as a genre, until I started to write my own book about Paris, and wondered about writers' insatiable appetite for the city.

My curiosity was partially motivated by my own reaction to the place. While researching *The Light of Paris*, I spent about six weeks there. Now, I know there is a difference between visiting a place for a day or two and attempting to live there, so I will admit my moments of amazement were tempered by the exhaustion of quotidian tasks like shopping for groceries and doing laundry. But mostly, my reaction was that Paris, for all the wonders it contains, is just a city. It has its pretty parts and its grimy parts, its rude citizens and its friendly ones, its nice museums and its tourist traps. It felt, to me, more similar to any other big city than different.

So if it is just another city, why are we obsessed with it? Why do we love writing—and reading—stories about Paris?

Armed with this question, I went to seventeen other women writers from the United States, England, and Ireland, and asked them about their personal experiences visiting and living in Paris. I wanted to know the stories behind the stories—I wanted to know what they really, honestly thought about the City of Light. *Et voilà*. Their clever and funny and dreamy and sad and thoughtful answers are collected here.

A few words on what this anthology does not do: I asked for very personal stories, so larger questions—of race, of politics, of religion—are largely absent. Also, the limitations I set on the contributors narrowed the field of potential contributors—bestselling women authors who had written books connected to Paris—quite a bit. When I looked at this Venn diagram in particular, but even considering books about Paris as a whole, I was startled to see how heavily female, heterosexual, and white both the writers and the stories are. This is particularly interesting given the number of books—including mine—that revolve around 1920s Paris, which had a hugely diverse community of artists and expats. As there is always something more to say about Paris itself, there are always more stories to explore about the people—all the people—who have made it into a place that occupies our hearts and imaginations so fully.

Despite the limitations I had designed, when I received the essays I was surprised by how different they are. Paris is an enormous and complex place, and every one of us had a wildly different experience there. Michelle Gable and I both had . . . how shall we say it . . . *difficult* times in Paris, though ultimately we both look back on our trips with fondness, and Michelle's story of her family's trip makes me smile whenever I think of it. But reading Meg Waite Clayton's or M.J. Rose's tours of the most delicious ways to spend your time in Paris would make anyone ache to go back (especially if you could have either one of them as a tour guide). If you are looking for a little romance, by the way, jump straight to their essays—those two know all about the City of Love.

If you aren't so much for the romance, Maggie Shipstead offers a beautiful and funny meditation on solitude in a city that seems devoted to lovers. The isolation of traveling abroad, especially in a country where you don't speak the language fluently, is a common experience, and one of the hardest parts of travel. But Maggie sees the value in that loneliness, in the way it both holds us back and cracks us open, and forces us to really experience and appreciate the place where we are.

And Julie Powell talks about how food can help us overcome that displacement of travel, how finding "your" restaurant or café or bar in a strange city can make it feel like home. (A word of advice: You might not want to read her essay when you are hungry, or by the end you will be so pleasantly dizzy from her lovely food descriptions that you will be deeply tempted to bite directly into a stick of European butter. Not that I'm speaking from experience.)

As different as our experiences were, our paths also crossed in unexpected ways. Many of the essays mention the Tuileries and Luxembourg Gardens, or the Louvre. But it's the smaller coincidences that are so pleasantly surprising. I can't say it ever occurred to me, on a trip to Paris, to seek out the police department, but both mystery writer Cara Black and historical author Lauren Willig do just that, albeit with quite different results. And Cara and British author Rachel Hore both write about the darker side of a city known for romance—Cara wondering where one might discover a body on those cobblestoned streets, and Rachel picturing a city under siege as she researched the Nazi occupation of Paris during World War II.

And while of course many of us did visit the Louvre, Susan Vreeland, whose novels explore the stories behind some of art's greatest works, shows us a side to the museum most of us will never see, breaking down the persistent stereotype of the un-friendly, unhelpful Parisian at the same time.

In fact, the Paris Tourism Board, with their recent campaign to get the French to be *un petit* bit friendlier to tourists, could take heart in many of the stories the contributors share here. In addition to Susan's experience, J. Courtney Sullivan's friendship with her French editor and her husband is a reminder that people are, after all, just people—and can be kind and funny and help-ful in the hardest of times. And Jennifer Scott's time living with a French family in Paris will make you long to be invited to din-ner at her home, where she uses everything she learned from them about elegance and grace and a gentler way of living.

Many of us went to Paris to research our books, but, as al-ways seems to happen with travel, got more than we bargained for. Paula McLain and Therese Anne Fowler both went to Paris for research—Paula was following in the footsteps of Ernest Hemingway and his first wife, Hadley, Therese in Zelda Fitzger-ald's. There, Paula learned that capturing the past is harder than it seems, and Therese learned that even Paris can't rescue us from ourselves, though it sure is a gorgeous place to try. And Cathy Kelly writes from the other side—of the books that made her fall in love with Paris, and the joy of finally coming to the city and actually being in the heart of all that glamor and intrigue and passion.

Because it turns out that there is something special about Paris after all. All that weight it carries, all the associations, can actually be a good thing—if you come at it with the right attitude.

Jennifer Coburn's mother-daughter trip to Paris didn't go quite as she had imagined. Instead, it offered her a chance to connect with her mother in a way she hadn't since she was a child. Megan Crane (aka romance novelist Caitlin Crews) wanted Paris to solve all her problems, and it did—by allowing her to see that she already had everything she needed. Ellen Sussman's passion for living in Paris hid the crumbling of her marriage, but it also taught her how to live richly and passionately and fully.

"My time in Paris," says Paula McLain in her essay, "was like no one else's ever." Paris is different for each of us. But when I read these stories, I feel connected to everyone else's experiences. Paris here becomes "commonplace" in the best sense of the word— something we all share. And though Julie Powell's Paris is not Jennifer Coburn's Paris is not M.J. Rose's Paris is not Michelle Gable's Paris, I can see that they are all related, can see pieces of my experience in theirs. I mentioned some of the ways in which these essays are full of delightfully serendipitous echoes, and that is the joy of Paris. When you go, you are in Hemingway's Paris and Victor Hugo's Paris, but you are also in Ellen Sussman's Paris and Paula McLain's Paris, and yet you are in a Paris all your own.

*Bon voyage.*

# A PARIS
# ALL YOUR OWN

⚜

# THIRTEEN WAYS OF LOOKING AT A FRENCH WOMAN

## J. Courtney Sullivan

### I. 1987

It begins, like all things, with my mother.

In our suburban Massachusetts neighborhood, full of Irish Catholics who throw block parties and summer cookouts, she believes that, in her heart, she is French. She collects Quimper pottery, wears silk scarves with the confidence of a native Parisian, and spritzes Chanel N°5 on the dog after a bath.

Her passion is inherited from her own mother, my grandmother, who to me seems every bit as glamorous as Catherine Deneuve. She subscribes to *W*, and when she's collected enough back issues, she bags them up and brings them over to our house. My grandmother is known for being the first person ever to jog in her neighborhood, long before there was such a thing as jogging attire—she did it in a trench coat. She goes into the city to get her hair done at a proper salon that costs a fortune instead of at some underwhelming beauty parlor closer to home. She, too, believes that French women are superior to us, not that she knows any French women. Her portals to that world are fashion magazines and Julia Child, whom she watches religiously on television, absorbing Child's thoughts on butter and wine, filling notebooks with her recipes. Notebooks we will find and cherish after my grandmother is gone.

## II. 1996

In high school French class, we watch the movies *Red*, *White*, and *Blue*, Kieślowski's *Three Colors* trilogy. On my own, I watch *Before Sunrise* approximately ninety-seven times. I want to be Juliette Binoche and Julie Delpy in equal measure, even though they are nothing alike. They are both French. Seemingly effortless in their beauty. Strong and commanding and flawlessly dressed, even at life's most depressing moments. I have that sense that if I just study them enough, I might become them through osmosis. I am fifteen. Nothing my mother does could possibly please me. But I realize that on this one point, she was correct: French women are spectacular in every way.

I love the language. I love my French teacher, who tells us one day, "Joy is happiness with no strings attached." Later, when almost all my French is forgotten, I will remember this.

## III. 2001

I announce that I plan to take a year off from college, horrifying my mother. I want to write and see the world. I would love to spend the year in France, but I don't have the guts, or the confidence for the language. I am twenty and I have never been outside the United States. As if to put a fine point on my naiveté, I declare that I will either move to London, or to Orlando, Florida, where I'll be employed at Disney World as part of a student work program. The program offers all kinds of positions. Some people even get to dress up as characters, perform in shows. I apply and am granted the job of fry cook. And so I choose London, where I work first as an intern at a literary agency, and later as a nanny for a family with three boys under the age of two.

I tell my friend Kirsty at the agency about my love of Paris, my urge to go. She says she knows Americans are crazy about it, but the place doesn't hold such allure for the English. Paris is for quick weekend jaunts, bachelorette parties, that sort of thing.

One long weekend, I finally go, and stay with a friend who is studying abroad there. We last saw each other at our casual college in the middle of nowhere, a place where pajama pants were considered appropriate dinner attire. But now I find that the city and all its glamor have made an impact on her. She is living as a lodger in the home of a Parisian book editor in the 16th arrondissement. She skips lunch each day and saves up to buy a Louis Vuitton clutch instead. (Though she confesses that once, in a fit of homesickness, she devoured a Big Mac. When she tells the story, she does not call McDonald's "McDonald's." She calls it, in perfectly accented French, *McDo*. Somehow even fast food seems more glamorous here.)

This is it. At last. The Paris the women of my family have

been dreaming about forever. I am the first of us to reach it. I get my picture taken in front of the Eiffel Tower but to my surprise I can't manage to feel much for it. I have seen too many pictures, maybe, imagined it too many times. I had a stronger reaction to Brussels a month before, perhaps because I never had a single expectation for Brussels.

My friend and I rush through the Louvre and Père Lachaise like commuters at Penn Station. She is a generous host, but she has seen all this already. What she really wants to do is what everyone our age in every city wants to do—go out, get drunk, meet boys. Who am I to argue?

I watch French women on the train, in the shops, sitting outside at sidewalk cafés. It is true, what I've always believed about their beauty, their style. It's a code I want to crack, though I don't actually converse with a single French person, except for a passing hello to the book editor, and a boy I kiss at a bar, also more or less in passing.

The next morning, as I board the Eurostar back to London, a text message appears: *I kiss you, I love you, I remember you all my life.*

It is ridiculous, over-the-top. A cartoon of what a Frenchman might say. I keep it like a souvenir until the phone is lost.

## IV. 2004

After graduation, I move to New York to become a writer. My first job is as an assistant at a beauty magazine, where I am a total fish out of water. But I find that everyone in this world worships French women as much as I do. I interview photographers and stylists. Their inspirations for looks are always French women from several decades ago. Brigitte Bardot, Anouk Aimée.

Between student loan debt and the rent on a shared shoe-box apartment, I am well aware that I'm too poor to even think about visiting Paris again any time soon. I go there in books. Books I really like, like Adam Gopnik's *Paris to the Moon*. Books I love, like Diane Johnson's *Le Divorce*. Silly books about beauty secrets that I take from the communal shelf at work after everyone else has gone home. Chief among them: *French Women Don't Get Fat*.

I don't read this as a guide, hoping to become the things I find in its pages. I read it like I am Margaret Mead watching the Samoans, or an alien just landing on planet Earth and taking a look around. I have nothing in common with the women described in the book, much as I admire them. I wear Nikes to the office. Not even ballet flats. I am an impossibly bad dresser. Though I spend my days writing about makeup, I don't really know how to apply it. I have, in fact, gotten a little bit fat.

## V. 2007

I get a job at the *New York Times*, doing research for an opinion columnist. I start writing for the paper, too. On the weekends, I work on my novel. The tools I use during the week seep into my fiction. I like to create a character not from nothing, but by building the emotions and the unknowable on top of what can be known. I want to get the details just right. So when I write a worm farmer, I interview worm farmers. Dollhouse aficionados and paramedics get the same treatment.

It is a total thrill, getting to peer into other people's worlds. The best part of the job.

## VI. 2010

My first novel, *Commencement*, is published. One day I get an e-mail from an editor in Paris named Marie. She wants to know if her small publishing house can have the French rights to the book.

There are agents to consult at moments like this. Negotiations to be made. But picture it: My book in French. I reply right away. Yes, of course Marie can have the rights.

## VII. 2010

Nearly a decade after my first trip to Paris, I get to go back. My boyfriend Kevin and I are house-sitting for friends in London, and we make a quick three-night detour to the City of Light. This time, I am determined to do it right. To see everything important, all the sights.

A year earlier, my mother finally got her chance to go. I ask her for travel tips and we copy her itinerary more or less to the letter. She warns us not to try to do everything. Enjoy it, move at a leisurely pace. But instead, we try to do everything. As with that first glimpse of the Eiffel Tower years earlier, we find that there is far less joy in the expected attractions than there is in the surprises—our hotel in the Latin Quarter, built on the remains of a thirteenth-century abbey; a party we stumble upon in the

grand courtyard of an art school, the students dancing and singing and showcasing their work. But some of the expected places
are incredible too. Versailles astonishes me. I could stay at the
piano bar at the Hôtel de Crillon for weeks. I think of how
beauty is such an important part of everyday life in Paris in a
way it is not in New York, as we sit in the Luxembourg Gardens
and watch children eating ice cream carved into the shape of
flowers.

We are, decidedly, tourists. As evidenced by the thick blue-
and-yellow copy of *Rick Steves Paris* that we carry everywhere we
go. A few times a day, I glimpse someone else carrying this book,
and we smile bashfully at each other, found out.

The taxi drivers can't understand my attempts at French.
They switch to English seconds after I open my mouth. I am kind
of relieved getting back to London, a city that has never seemed
intimidating to me.

## VIII. 2012

*Commencement* is released in France and becomes a bestseller
there. In French, it is called *Les Debutantes.*

I am beginning a new novel, my third, called *The Engagements.* From the start, I know that one of the main characters
will be a glamorous Parisian woman. A woman I will never be,
but have always admired from afar.

I begin by interviewing Parisian transplants to Boston and
New York. I ask them everything. One of the things I cherish
most about being a writer is this: If you were just to say to a person,

"Tell me everything about yourself," they might balk. But if you say, "I am a writer, tell me so that I can make a story from it," they will almost always do it.

The women I talk to make excellent subjects because they've lived in both worlds. I decide my character will be the same. A Parisian transplant to New York, so that I can see what my own city looks like through her eyes. I give her a name. Delphine.

My interview subjects mention the small irritations of American life—too much air-conditioning, the ubiquity of Starbucks. And big ones, too—how strangers cling to false familiarity, making promises to get together again, but never keeping them. Helicopter parents. The gym-obsessed. The way, at dinner parties, people tend to pair off and talk to only one person instead of having a lively group discussion.

The things they miss most include good bread, Avene Hydrance Optimale face cream. French *Elle. Paris Match.*

I learn that in their kitchens in Paris, there are always cubes instead of grains in the sugar bowl. That pastis is never kept in the fridge. That as a term of endearment, one's mother might call one *mon tourterelle*, "my turtledove." They tell me that in Paris, if you meet someone for coffee but don't feel like the caffeine, you might order a *citron pressé*—lemonade. They tell me of a French wedding tradition in which a bride and groom hide in a broom closet, waiting to be found by their guests.

I want to know Delphine's Paris. It seems only responsible to return there for research. Kevin comes with me again. We are recently engaged. I know exactly where I want to go—Montmartre and the rue Cler, the two neighborhoods I have decided will be most important to Delphine.

Through a company called Paris Walks, I hire a private guide, Brad, who takes us around Montmartre, where he lives. I have been before, but now I notice new things. A luthier's shop with violins hanging in the window. A small vineyard that was tended by Benedictine monks in the twelfth century. The old *tabacs* turned late-night grocery stores run by North African immigrants. The astonishing view of Paris from the outdoor tables at Chez Pommette. The artist studios built high up in the garrets of old houses, where the light is best. An ivy-covered brick house on rue Cauchois, with tall white shutters and bright red geraniums in the window boxes.

Before, in Paris, I was always self-conscious. *Did I sound like a stupid American? Was my accent atrocious?* But in the role of writer, I'm too curious to care.

Kevin and I go to hear a violin soloist play in the Église de Saint-Germain-des-Prés. We stumble upon a summer carnival at the edge of the Tuileries Gardens late one night—at picnic tables, people eat crêpes and cotton candy, and drink wine. Children jump on trampolines and scream with mock terror on the rides.

On a Sunday morning, we go to a bustling outdoor market beneath the elevated train tracks on the boulevard de Grenelle. Fruit merchants sell enormous tomatoes and eggplant, ripe cherries, artichokes, seven different kinds of mushrooms. One stall has thirty kinds of olives in wooden bins, and any herb or nut you could imagine. There are men selling fish and meat, all of it displayed beautifully, presentation as important as quality. At a *fromagerie*, a father-daughter pair offers two dozen wheels of cheese, which they slice and wrap in pale blue paper. Flower stalls burst with roses and calla lilies. I eat three tiny beignets while I watch old ladies do their shopping for the week.

This is the trip on which I fall in love with Paris. Not Paris as I'd imagined it, but Paris as it is.

## IX. 2012

I write all of Delphine's chapters in a small guest bedroom at Kevin's mother's house in Des Moines, Iowa. It's about as un-Parisian a setting as you can get, but the memories are fresh and I can transport myself there in an instant.

I haven't yet met my French editor, Marie, but we have a lively e-mail correspondence, in which we talk about books and life. In October, I send her the manuscript, worried about whether I've gotten Delphine right.

I've set a scene on the rue de Passy, and it turns out this is the street where Marie grew up. A good omen. Overall, she says I have captured Delphine well. I want her to correct me where she can, and so she points out a few things I have missed.

As I revise, I send Marie questions and she dutifully replies. I ask if the French really eat *steak frites*. (Yes, she says, but that name is just for tourists. The French would specify what kind of steak. They would say, "*entrecôte frite.*") Would Delphine and her husband eat dinner at Le Florimond? (Yes.) Is it true that French women never drink wine when it is not accompanied by food? (No.) What kind of cigarettes would Delphine's mother-in-law smoke? (Gitanes.) I want to know which newspaper Delphine would read. Marie says she could spend hours explaining the difference between *Le Monde* and *Liberation*, but let's just leave it at *Le Monde*.

## X. 2013

In April, I finally get to meet Marie and her business partner/husband Jean-Pierre, when I go to Paris to promote my second novel, *Maine*. April in Paris, just like the song.

I am coming from a similar promotional trip in Vienna, where I curl my hair every morning for the first and only time in my life. I have purchased new clothes. A pink DVF sweater that zips up the back. A blue Marc Jacobs dress covered in tiny white polka dots. Nude heels. No one here has to know that at home I spend my days writing in yoga pants or, at best, worn-out old jeans.

The plan is for Kevin to meet me on the second day in France. The night before I leave Vienna, I receive a rush of text messages from my family back home in Boston. There has been a bombing at the marathon finish line. My mother was standing right there, posting pictures to Facebook just minutes before. It's over an hour before we learn that she is safe. I get to talk to her on the phone only briefly, in the middle of the night. I tell her I will come home immediately and she says, "Don't you dare."

It feels wonderful to sit in interviews, discussing my novel, with brilliant French journalists. But it also feels strange, given the circumstances back home.

I just want Kevin to get there, and I'll be okay, I think. Then his flight is cancelled. Boston is put on lockdown while the police search for the killers. I stay up all night watching coverage on the news. I sit on the floor of my hotel room and eat a hatbox of macarons from Arnaud Delmontel, a welcome gift from Jean-Pierre and Marie. Three days into my stay, Jean-Pierre asks if I've tried the macarons yet. I say they are delicious and report that I have eaten them all. He laughs, like it's impossible. But really. I have eaten them all.

Kevin's flight gets cancelled again the next night, and the next. I follow Boston on the news. Surreal to see it in all the newspaper headlines, on the other side of the ocean.

Marie and I eat several meals together. She is wonderful. Funny and cool and so, so French. She gives me notes on where to go shopping, and I do. I buy two dresses in a little shop, and shoes at the Bon Marché. A rite of passage. I am alone a lot. I spend hours walking the city one day. I sit alone at an outdoor café, eating a tomato salad because I am a vegetarian now. So not French. Marie tells me it is actually considered unpatriotic in France to not eat meat. All the same, she takes me to lunch at a tiny, amazing vegan restaurant near her apartment. She tells me she doesn't care for New York, but she loves LA.

I am supposed to appear in a bookstore on the final night. I give the driver directions in French and he understands me. A rush of joy. A friend who has moved to Paris is there, and Brad, the tour guide. Marie's sister comes, and so do a couple dozen others.

Afterward, we go back to Marie's apartment for a little party. I am in such a swirl of emotion. Happy, but so sad for my hometown. Relieved that my mother is unharmed, but worried for so many others. Missing Kevin, wishing he could have come. How often, home in Boston, I dreamed of Paris. And now I am in Paris dreaming of home. At one point in the evening, I start to cry. Marie points me to her bedroom. We sit on the bed together, talking. When I say, "I'm ruining the party," she just shrugs and says we'll sit awhile longer. She brings me a glass of wine.

## XI. 2014

For some time now, ever since Kevin's three missed flights, Marie has teased me that I've made him up. A few days after our wedding, she writes to say that she was thinking of me that day, and to ask how it went. I write her back, attach some photos. She replies, *Thank you for the pictures! Gorgeous dress! And indeed this man that you hired for the pictures and that you name Kevin seems very nice.*

They meet at last when we return to France for something called the Festival America in Vincennes, a close suburb of Paris, the last stop on the Métro. It's an incredible event, full of American authors and audiences that are completely French. Americans so often approach the French in sweeping terms—*they're all like this, they think it's awful when you do that.* The Festival America is all about their ideas about us. The panels I'm on have names like "Whatever Happened to the American Dream?"

After the festival, in Paris, Kevin and I go on a tour of the opera house. We go to a local market afterward and cobble together a lunch from the stalls. We stand before a man selling salt out of glass bowls. Row after row of gorgeous salts, tinged pink, beige, green.

That night, we have dinner at Marie and Jean-Pierre's apartment. It turns out Kevin and Jean-Pierre love lots of the same bands. Kevin plays chess with their young son, even though they can't say a word to each other. We drink many bottles of wine. We stay until after two.

## XII. 2015

When I see on the television that Paris is under attack, I think of Marie and Jean-Pierre, their children. I write to them immediately. When they reply, I am filled with such relief. The world is so uncertain, so severe. But at least they are safe, our friends.

## XIII.

In *The Engagements*, Delphine's father is the piano player at the Hôtel de Crillon. The ivy-covered house on rue Cauchois is her home. Lots of little memories I've collected make it into the story. The summer carnival, the luthier shop. Ice cream in the shape of flowers. Arnaud Delmontel macarons. Even those three beignets I ate at the outdoor market. (Though Marie corrected me. A French woman would never eat three. I should change it to one.)

Paris was once a place that existed only in my dreams. Even after I had seen it in person a time or two, I couldn't really see it. The fiction writer's paradox: Sometimes things become clearer, more real, when you view them through the eyes of a character. Not looking at, but looking *as*.

When Delphine first appears on the page, she's wearing a blue belted shirtwaist with black flowers swirling this way and that. It's a detail imported from home, the shirtwaist handed down from my grandmother to my mother to me. My grandmother never made it to Paris, but I like to think that it would please her, the thought of a real Parisian woman, strolling up the hill in Montmartre, wearing her favorite dress.

⚜ ⚜ ⚜

**J. Courtney Sullivan** is the author of the *New York Times* bestselling novels *Commencement, Maine,* and *The Engagements. Maine* was named a Best Book of the Year by *TIME* magazine, and a *Washington Post* Notable Book for 2011. *The Engagements* was one of *People* magazine's Top Ten Books of 2013 and an *Irish Times* Best Book of the Year. It is soon to be a major motion picture produced by Reese Witherspoon and distributed by Fox 2000, and has been translated into seventeen languages. Her latest novel is *Saints for All Occasions*. She lives in Brooklyn, New York.

### Say bonjour:
jcourtneysullivan.com
Facebook: /JCourtneySullivan
Twitter: @JCourtSull

### The Paris Book:
*The Engagements*

### I write about Paris because . . .
Reading and/or writing about Paris is the most affordable way to visit a city that I'd happily fly off to once a month if money were no object.

### Favorite Paris moment:
Drinking a bottle of Champagne with my husband in the courtyard of the Louvre sometime after midnight.

### Favorite book about Paris:
*Le Divorce* by Diane Johnson perfectly captures Paris through the eyes of an admiring outsider, who becomes an insider with time. *Americans in Paris*, an anthology edited by Adam Gopnik, shows the Paris of Mark Twain, Edith Wharton, Elizabeth Bishop, and others. It's wonderful and transporting.

*Song that reminds you of Paris:*

Frank Sinatra, singing "April in Paris." Half my fantasies about the city were born from listening to this song over and over again.

*Favorite non-Paris travel destination:*

The west of Ireland.

*In Paris, you must . . .*

Walk all over with no plan in mind, and don't shut your eyes for a second. You will never see a place more beautiful.

⚜ ⚜ ⚜

# TOO MUCH PARIS

*Michelle Gable*

"We're going to Paris," my mom announced.

She said it with confidence, swagger, and the hard-earned smugness of having raised three successful kids, to say nothing of her status as Best Grandma Ever. You didn't tell Gam-Gam no.

"It's a milestone year," she said. "You're turning forty. Your father will be seventy and *your book is coming out*. It takes place *in Paris*. We must celebrate."

*A Paris Apartment*, my debut novel, was about to launch. Having sweated through cancelled contracts, a failed bidding war between publishers, and too many rejected manuscripts to count, the book's publication still felt gauzy, vaporous, like it might dissolve on contact. Now my mom wanted to jinx my lifelong dream with a harebrained jaunt to Paris?

"I don't know," I said. "Our summer is packed. Camps. Work trips. With All-Stars, the girls play softball into July."

"We're going," she declared, the decision long since made.

"But I was just *in* Paris."

"For work, which doesn't count. Come on, Michelle, it's Paris!"

"But, Mom . . ."

"IT'S PARIS."

The woman had a point.

⚜

The first problem: Though I'd been to Paris several times, my husband hadn't. And he wasn't keen on going.

"I'm not a meathead," Dennis said, trying to tell our friends Karen and Tom why he wasn't hot on the idea. "I enjoy museums and culture. I loved Florence and Milan and Prague."

"So *why*?" Karen pressed. "What's the problem?"

My best friend since junior high, Karen was well schooled in Dennis's immutability, as well as the oligarchy that is my mom. She understood my cramped position between them.

"Now we have kids," Dennis explained.

"Don't we all," Karen said.

"I'm not spoiling them with a trip to Europe. Plus, there are other ways I'd rather spend my money and PTO."

"For instance: golf," I said, and rolled my eyes.

Because why Paris when you could agonize over your short game?

"Yes, that's part of it . . ."

"Listen, I like golf as much as the next guy"—Tom interjected. This was a stone fact, as Dennis *was* the next guy, and they both loved golf, frequently together—"but nothing, not even golf, compares to Paris. If you pass up the opportunity, you'll regret it."

And so Dennis agreed. Due to Tom's endorsement, or my incessant pleas, or simply because my husband is the greatest.

Whatever the reason, we were headed to Paris. A good thing, too, since I'd bought the tickets weeks earlier.

⚜

The second problem: telling our daughters. At ages eight and ten, they didn't get that Paris is *Paris*.

Big sister Paige was neutral, her trademark style.

"Can I use your iPad on the plane?" she asked.

"Um, sure?" I said.

She nodded her agreement, never to speak of it again.

"I can't go," little sister Georgia proclaimed. "They have mimes there."

"But also mustaches," I said.

She contemplated this for a minute before declaring, "Sold."

As Paige dreamed of ways to clutter my iPad with terrible games, Georgia wrote down her must-see Paris landmarks. At least one of my kids understood the importance of our journey (*this is Paris, people!*). On the other hand, Georgia's lists were notoriously tough, never solvable with something as easy as Amazon Prime or a trip to Target. For her birthday she had asked for the resurrection of two grandparents and one cat. Lord knew what she expected from the City of Light.

Within a breath, the school year ended, All-Stars wrapped up, and it was time for the Big Trip. Even Paige scrounged up a base level of excitement. We were going to Paris! How lucky were we?

Dennis and I flew out first, with my parents scheduled to

bring the girls a few days later. Gam-Gam and Gramps insisted on business class and so the girls would likewise fly in style. Since I refused to cramp up in coach while my elementary schoolers fully reclined, I used miles from my travel-intense day job to upgrade, despite knowing Dennis would find it extravagant in the extreme. And so I procrastinated on breaking the news.

"Business class?" Dennis squawked.

We stood at the gate, boarding passes in hand. So I didn't so much "break the news" as "wait for him to notice." Luckily, he'd been busy.

"We're flying business class?"

"I told you that," I said, the wobble in my voice selling me out from the start.

"No. You didn't."

"I used miles." I sniffed. "Anyway, I'm not flying coach if the girls aren't!"

"THE GIRLS AREN'T IN COACH?"

"Gam-Gam insisted . . ."

"*I've* never even flown business."

"Don't forget my DVT! I have a history of blood clots!"

People gawped, and for good reason. Who complained about business class? Accountants and military kids like Dennis, that's who.

Suddenly my phone rang, and right on time. My agent was calling with news that *A Paris Apartment* was a national best-seller. I grinned and blocked out Dennis's kvetching. Learning that my little Paris book was a bestseller while *en route to Paris*?

Forget surly husbands and unappreciative kids. Our trip would be spectacular. It had to be. My insides jumped at the thought.

❧

We arrived in Paris midday.

It was hot—murderously hot. Flashing signs warned people to drink water and stay indoors. After a snafu with the keys (conducted in stilted, half-understood French), we stepped into our apartment. And it was glorious.

The home was in the 16th arrondissement. It had wood floors, white walls, and an Eiffel Tower view. My second novel was due in October and I envisioned hours toiling away in the writing nook. It had a writing nook! (I never used the nook.)

As I unpacked, Dennis fiddled with the television.

"Should we go?" he said after checking the leaderboard of one golf tournament or another.

"Um . . . ?" I weighed my words. "Are you planning to . . . change?"

We were tourists but I wanted to blend in—a tough sell. Forget his über-American personage (tall, athletic, handsome, blond), Dennis was sporting black Adidas and khaki *shorts*. Shorts, for the love of croissants.

"We don't want to look like Americans . . ." I stuttered.

"We *are* American," he said.

"You could get pants? Pink skinny trousers maybe? They're everywhere!"

Dennis didn't even bother to roll his eyes. He grabbed his wallet and headed toward the stairs.

We (read: Gam-Gam) had chosen the apartment due to its location. The neighborhood was tony, but charming and centrally located. It sat only a few blocks from the Métro, which would've been spectacular had the station not been closed until October.

"Super convenient," Dennis said, parroting my mother's oft-repeated phrase as we stared at the sign. A sole drop of sweat clung to his brow.

Trocadéro was the next closest stop, and almost a mile away. Uphill. In 100-degree weather. More eating for me, I reasoned. The girls would have to deal because the only whine allowed in Paris came in a bottle or by the glass.

Dennis and I spent the next two days exploring the (steamy, scorching) city. We visited a cemetery, museums, the Moulin Rouge. We ate steak tartare and drank local wine. To witness the white-domed splendor of the Sacré-Coeur we hiked 1,000 stairs, in 1,000 degrees, with 1,000 other people.

*The girls will hate this*, I thought, but shoved the idea away. I'd been talking up Paris for months. If we couldn't have fun in the greatest city in the world, what did that say about us? Everyone would love Paris, dammit. We *had* to love Paris. It was time to put on my game face and stop Googling nearby resorts we could escape to.

On our last night together before the gang rolled in, Dennis and I dined at La Coïncidence, a neighborhood joint that was lovely and quaint and clattering with French voices. The plates were plastic, the glasses Woody Woodpecker, the food simple but divine. When the waitress approached, she addressed us in rapid-fire French. We pretended to understand.

By the time we left, we were grinning, laughing, having bona fide "fun." At last, the vacation had found its groove. Everything was on the ascent.

But then . . . the girls showed up. And as all humankind understands, the situation doesn't improve when the kids arrive. Sometimes it even gets worse.

⚜

"Hey," Paige said as they walked through the front door.

She flopped onto the couch, demonstrably thrilled to see us.

"Calm down," I joked.

Paige rolled her eyes and then closed them.

"It's hot," she said. "Too hot for seeing."

Dennis and I exchanged hugs with my parents.

*Yes, the flight was wonderful.*

*What a beautiful apartment!*

*It is very hot.*

Georgia waddled in last and late, her definitive calling card. Imagine if every time you entered a room, palpable relief surged through the crowd. That's life as Georgia.

"Here," she said and thrust a notebook at me. "Read it."

She'd pushed her business-class eye mask high on her fore-head, *Fraggle Rock* hair spouting over the top.

"Is this your list?" I said, and opened the cover.

"Yes. I'm so tired."

Georgia lurched over to lean against Gam-Gam. Despite having taken an overnight flight with the girls, my mother didn't mind playing lamppost. Then and always, she was a wonder.

Meanwhile, I reviewed Georgia's Parisian requirements.

*To see,* she had written in princess cursive, *1. Gustave Eiffel's apartment. 2. Versailles. 3. Mona Lisa.*

I smiled. Moppet had done her homework, and the bar was low.

"This is fantastic," I said, and showed Dennis. "We could walk to the Eiffel Tower right now. Look! You can see it through the window!"

"No thanks," Georgia said and slid away from Gam-Gam.

She shuffled across the parquet floors and fell onto the couch beside her sister. As Paige shoved at her with one foot, Georgia nestled in closer and lowered the eye mask.

"No napping!" I yelped. "Was the flight not enough rest for you slackers? Come on! Look alive! You're in Paris!"

"They watched television the whole time," Gam-Gam said. "All night long."

"Listen," my dad said. "I'll shower and then we're going outside. You have thirteen minutes."

We agreed. Or rather, Gramps left the room before anyone could argue.

After cleaning up and coaxing two floppy girls to their feet, we dragged them toward the stairs and out onto rue Raynouard. At once the sticky air overtook us. I lifted damp strands of hair from my neck.

We'd walked one half block when the air seemed to change, and not because of the weather. When we turned our collective heads, we found Georgia several paces behind. She was frozen in place, a scowl on her face. I glanced at her feet. She'd stepped in a pile of poo.

"Oh, shit," my dad said with one of his tight-lipped, grimacing chuckles.

"Exactly," Dennis said.

Georgia's eyes burned hot and red and watery.

"Georgie, just wipe it off," I said. "It's no big deal. Quite Parisian, as a matter of fact! People don't clean up after their dogs. I mentioned it in my book! This is going to make a great story. It's perfect when you think about it!"

"Seriously, Mom?" Paige said, appropriately.

Good lord, I was trying to dress up actual shit. *I swear, girls, even the poop has meaning in Paris.*

Georgia continued to scrutinize me with her cutting green gaze. After a solid six minutes, she removed the offending shoe and wiped it on a nearby building. A businessman whipped around to confirm what he'd seen and reestablish his distaste for Americans.

"I'm done," Georgia said and turned toward the apartment. "Let me know when we're leaving for London."

Gam-Gam went to fetch her. She was the only one who stood a chance.

Somehow, much later, all six of us reached the Eiffel Tower, and we have the family picture to prove it. In the photograph, I am smiling; Dennis is not. One daughter appears smug while the other clutches a notebook, looking very much like she's just stepped in shit.

⚜

The line for the Eiffel Tower elevator was approximately forty-seven hours long and so we tramped 669 steps (Paige counted) to the second platform for our city view. After snapping a few pictures, we turned to go back down.

"Gustave Eiffel's apartment?" Georgia stabbed an angry finger at her book. "I wrote it down. So where is it?"

"At the top. But we're not standing in another line," Dennis said, matter-of-fact.

What the heck? He didn't even *false promise* that we'd go another time, or offer ice cream, or suggest an alternative bribe. Was he trying to parent in a foreign country without our usual crutches? I shot him a glare, which he expertly ignored.

"You made me walk all this way," Georgia growled. "I stepped in crap. I saw two clowns *and a mime . . .*"

"That mime was creepy," Paige agreed.

"And now I don't even get to see Gustave Eiffel's apartment?"

"Sweetheart . . ." I started.

I looked to Dennis for backup, but he and Paige were already out of sight.

"We'll try to visit his apartment later in the week," I said. "Come on, let's get ice cream before they close."

"What time do they close?" Georgia asked, one brow arched.

I checked my fake watch.

"Seven after four? Let's hurry!"

I hated how pandering I sounded. It's not my parenting style, and, in fact, two weeks before I'd accused Georgia of faking sick during district playoffs. I told her to "jog it off," in catcher's gear, when "it" turned out to be pneumonia and a 105-degree fever. No one would accuse my kids of being coddled, business-class upgrades notwithstanding.

"Do you want to hold my hand?" I asked then, on the second platform of the Eiffel Tower, in the best city in the world.

"No," she said. "Not even a little."

But Georgia followed me . . . a small miracle. I got the sense we'd need a lot more of them to make it through this trip.

❦

After the (sweaty, oh so sweaty) Eiffel ascent, we congregated outside the Trocadéro, where Dennis and the girls dipped their feet in water so green it glowed.

Look, I understood the desperation to cool off. Even I'd succumbed to wearing shorts. But the Palais de Chaillot had been built for the 1937 World's Fair, and I doubted anyone had changed the water since. High temps were no excuse for contracting hepatitis B. As they frolicked, I pulled out my phone and Googled "horrible family vacations why."

That evening it rained. I wasn't happy, exactly, but it'd be nice not to sweat through three outfits a day. And maybe the storm would carry something more. As tourists, as a family, we were grouchy, snippy, floundering on the wrong side of the world. Might a change in weather change our circumstances? Or at least our attitudes? A mom could dream.

Socked together beneath umbrellas, we clambered a few blocks to a nearby bistro and coaxed them into feeding us at the ungodly, un-Parisian time of six o'clock. The girls had been up forty-eight hours straight and we were all delirious with hunger and acute peevishness. As the rest of the city only began to think about dinner, we shared endless plates of food and bottles of wine, rain clacking against the windows.

Georgia tried olives and sweetbreads (NO ONE TELL HER!) while Paige ravaged the bread wolverine-style, ripping out the soft centers before discarding the baguette carcasses onto the table. I drank and ate more than I should've, but Paris is no place for moderation. That night we slept soundly, the rain and wine and conversation a blanket, a salve for our cranky little hearts.

⚜

Whatever lessons we'd learned evaporated by morning.

Instead of basking in the food and lights and uninterrupted family time of Paris, we woke with determination and set about assaulting the guidebook landmarks: Place de la Concorde, the Arc de Triomphe, Napoleon's Tomb, Sainte-Chapelle, Saint-Sulpice, and the Grande Roue at the Jardin des Tuileries.

We also canvassed the museums, landmarks like the Musée Rodin, which earned high marks thanks to a well-placed butt statue. Not so much the Musée d'Orsay, where Georgia assumed a yogic *Savasana*, center floor, oblivious to the tourists leaping over her splayed body.

"You've been begging me all summer to see Katy Perry," I hissed. "Done. We'll go and I'll sit beside you and complain the whole time."

"That works," she said. "Anyway, I'm better at ignoring you than you are at ignoring me."

Touché, *petit monstre*. Touché.

Who could forget the Musée de l'Orangerie, with Paige in head-to-toe Chargers gear, doing knee-ups beside *Les Nymphéas*? After Monet's famed water lilies, we visited the Galeries Lafayette, where Paige fell in love with a red Dolce & Gabbana pochette.

"You're not into accessories," I reminded her as the tears gathered.

Paige was supposed to be my sporty kid, nonfancy to the core. The swanky sister and her dad were at the Grévin wax museum, and Gam-Gam and I had left to shop and sip bubbly at the Champagne bar. We'd assumed Paige would stick to her customary routine: sit quietly for two hours until we remembered she was there.

But instead my daughter stood beneath the Galeries' grand, kaleidoscopic, Belle Époque ceiling *weeping about a purse*. This was a girl whose favorite "outfit" involved three-year-old soccer shorts and a freebie Padres baseball cap.

What was with these kids? Or my husband, for that matter? Even Gramps hadn't made a snarky comment in days and, what's more, had the nerve to call the girls "good travelers." That he resorted to such a desperate and egregious lie meant he felt the strain of the trip, too. Thank God for Gam-Gam, the only reasonable one among us.

"I must have it!" Paige continued to cry. "It looks great on me!"

As I myself was halfway to tears, I texted a picture to my sister, my lifeline to the regular world.

"Isn't this ridiculous?" I wrote. "D&G! For Paige! When I can't even get her to bathe more than twice a week!"

"I would've gotten it," my sister responded. "Paige is right. U R mean."

Then Georgia strolled up, right on time, and immediately launched into her own tirade about fine leather goods.

"You don't even like to accessorize, PAIGE," she said, spitting out her sister's name like a swear word. "And when is it my turn?"

Thank God for the Champagne bar, otherwise Maman would've lost her *merde*.

Through it all I couldn't decide if I was being too hard on the girls, or not hard enough. They'd been easy kids since day one— good nappers, good students, good athletes, good restaurant patrons. Georgia slept eight hours straight her first night alive.

"My babies sleep," I told the panicked nurse. "That's what they do."

Now, in Paris, my angels were sulky and cantankerous. On the other hand, so was I. Were my behavioral expectations sufficiently child-size? Or were they better suited to slick, assured world travelers unaffected by time zones and foreign customs? I was starting to think that maybe the problem was me.

On day who-knows, on the morning of lord-help-me, we took a tour of Paris's gothic architecture, an assured recipe for gripes. Even *I* would've preferred a Katy Perry concert. But, you know, Gam-Gam.

Alas, to my great shock, the guide entranced the girls with her melodic voice and gothic tales. Georgia gaped at the rose windows and flying buttresses. She begged for more stories of revolution.

The ever-diffident Paige called at least one thing "cool." Afterward we got ice cream at the famed Berthillon on Île Saint-Louis. Everyone was smiling. *Even Dennis.* The sun shone in the exact right amount.

Finally, we'd figured out Paris. The city wasn't about doing every possible thing, but finding what spoke to us. And wouldn't you know? I didn't Google "family vacations horrible" once that day. It's no wonder these places made it into my second book.

That night we took a boat tour on the Seine and witnessed the pink-and-purple magic of a Parisian sunset. When night fell completely, the Eiffel Tower began its glittering show. We stood together, marveling, and for one glorious moment no one uttered a complaint of any kind. We felt like our usual selves. In other words, the luckiest people alive.

❧

With two days left in Paris, we were 0 for 3 on Georgia's list. Luckily, my mother had arranged a tour of Versailles. Always thinking, that Gam-Gam.

Our guide was charming and knowledgeable, albeit a little too knowledgeable if you had an inquisitive eight-year-old and didn't care to bring affairs, murders, or miscarriages down to the third-grade level.

"How you say . . . the baby comes out? With blood? Dead?" *[Guide makes sweeping motion near groin.]*

"Sometimes babies aren't born?!" Georgia cried. "They just *come out of you*? Mommy!"

"Christ," my dad muttered. "This is not going well."

"This company is geared toward children!" my mom chirped. "Promise!"

The tour was of the gardens, but we planned to check out the palace itself. A doomed plan, in the end. We arrived at nine o'clock, and even if we got in line immediately, we wouldn't make it inside by closing. Yet another strikeout for Georgia. And just ask her softball coach—Georgia does not abide striking out.

Georgia shuffled along begrudgingly (*"No Golden palace?!"*) as the guide regaled us with the gardens' history and mythological origins. It was an impressive tour, but long, oh so long. As we walked, the weather cooled. My teeth began to chatter. At some point along the way, Georgia commandeered the guide's sweater and scarf. To maintain harmony, we repeatedly placated the girls with hot chocolate and crêpes. They had gobs of Nutella on their shirts and in their hair.

Shortly after noon, we stood shivering in the mist as the guide described the statue before us ("How you say . . . he had sex with her by force?").

"Ah. *The Rape of Persephone*," Dennis said in his sly drawl, scratching his chin in faux-contemplation. "Geared toward children indeed."

I couldn't help but snort.

"All right, that's enough," Gramps said as he chucked a fistful of euros at the guide. *"Au revoir.* Have a good day."

"So I gather . . ." Georgia started as we scurried toward the train station.

*I gather.* That kid kills me, on her best and worst days.

"I gather we're not actually seeing Versailles?" she asked. "Just like we didn't see Gustave Eiffel's apartment? Close, but not quite."

"Sorry, sweetheart," I said, no false promises this time. "The line is too long."

"The line is too long." She sighed. "The line is always too flippin' long."

❧

It was our last day in Paris.

The girls slept past eleven, exhausted from the sightseeing and bellyaching. As they snoozed and Dennis deciphered a French telecast golf tournament, I hit the rue de Passy for a solo shopping trip. Finally, a chance for *me* to cry over expensive purses.

I returned to the apartment well after lunch. Everyone was awake and Dennis looked ticked.

"So we're not going to the Louvre?" he said.

"Were we supposed to?" I asked meekly.

We didn't have specific plans, but I understood the question. Though I'd seen the Mona Lisa, Dennis hadn't. You couldn't go to Paris and *skip the Louvre.* They'd probably revoke your passport for such a crime against culture.

"I guess not," he grumbled.

I frowned. Poor guy. He was enduring this stress-riddled trip too, but at least I'd wanted to go in the first place. Dennis had come to Paris for me, and for the girls. And he'd asked exactly nothing in return.

"Well, it *is* late," I said and looked at my phone. "Almost three o'clock."

We were supposed to meet my parents in the 11th arrondissement at seven. Due to the closed Métro situation, this required our prescribed one-mile walk, three separate trains, and then another walk. In other words, it was a slog.

"Getting to the Louvre before dinner is aggressive," I said.

I glanced toward Georgia, who looked at me with eyes wide and wounded, worse than if I'd told her she'll never play professional baseball.

"But I can do aggressive," I said. "Some might say I'm known for it."

Screw it. Georgia needed a hit. We all did.

"Ladies! Dennis! Grab your shoes. We have a date with the Mona Lisa."

Georgia squealed and leapt to her feet, the fastest she'd ever set herself into motion. The laws of physics had been breached.

"You want to swing by the Louvre before dinner?" Dennis balked.

"It sounds ridiculous, but yes."

"And then meet your parents on the opposite end of the city?"

"Again. Ridiculous. But yes. My mom insists, and after everything she's done . . ."

"Fine," he said, ever the sport, ever the number-one guy. He slipped on his Adidas. "What's the place called again? The restaurant?"

"Bistrot Paul Bert?"

Dennis leveled his gaze.

"Bistrot Paul Bert," he repeated with a sigh. "All I can say is that Paul Bert had better be the best fucking restaurant in all of Paris."

⚜

The next day we left for London.

As we chugged along, I imagined the weight of Paris and its expectations floating away. I would've felt happy, borderline relieved, if not for the eight-year-old crying beside me. Paris gave us a parting shot.

The night before, as Georgia crawled into bed for the final time, news broke that the San Diego Padres had traded her favorite player, Chase Headley, to the Yankees.

"The Padres ruined Paris for me!" she'd say even now.

"Welcome to being a San Diego sports fan," Paige might tell her in response.

Now, on the train out of Paris, Georgia was working on another list—candidates for her new favorite baseball player. With any luck, for the Padres and for her, it'd result in a better average than the one with Gustave Eiffel and Versailles.

I turned toward Paige.

"So, what'd you think of Paris?" I asked. "Did you like it?"

She shrugged her in Paige way.

"It was cool," she said.

"What was your favorite part?"

She contemplated this for a minute.

"The plane," she said. "The best part was definitely the plane. Will we take the same one home?"

❦

Summer ended. School resumed. Friends wanted to know about Paris because of course they did.

"I'm glad we went," I said, and found this increasingly true, "but we preferred London."

London was our jam. Harry Potter and *Lion King* and the Buckingham Palace state rooms. Also, the English helped. And the lowered expectations. We weren't expecting it to be *Paris*.

"A memorable trip," I'd say. "Though not necessarily 'fun.'"

"Oh, sweetie," one friend said. "Of course it wasn't fun. You didn't take a vacation. You *traveled*."

Damn, she was right.

Everyone knows vacationing with kids is nothing more than "same shit, different place." And while we were a tad ambitious with our unique brand of traveling sideshow, we went abroad. We saw stuff. Two countries, to be specific. It'd qualify as the trip of a lifetime for most. Our journey wasn't "fun." But it was worth it.

"Oh yes, we've seen Paris," my girls can say from now until forever. "Mom wanted to throttle us all, but wasn't it *très grande*?"

I remembered the family trips we took when I was a kid. We visited hot spots like Moab, Utah, and its grossly trumped-up "Canyonlands by night" (e.g., a flashlight on the side of a mountain). We saw every state in the American West as we rolled around in the back of a diesel Suburban, *Rain Man* playing on a jerry-rigged VCR. We'd never forget Willie Nelson ("On the road again . . ."), my mom's *Passport to Your National Parks*, or my dad's fixation on "making good time."

*You can use the bathroom in Nevada, or in Utah, but not both.*

*I know I was speeding, Officer, but as you can see, my kids are obnoxious.*

These things, the fabric of a family. And good fodder when the kids are grown.

Many months after we returned, the Travel Channel featured a Paris-themed show. Dennis and I smiled as we relived the places we'd seen, and the ones we wanted to see but had missed.

"Next time," Dennis said.

There'd be a next time? Who would've guessed?

The show concluded with a promise to end the much-debated topic: "What's the best restaurant in Paris?" Old Michelle would've written it down, but I didn't even look for a pen. We'd find our own best restaurant, *thank you very much*. On our own time.

But then, right there on television, decreed by folks who'd seen and eaten everything—the city's best restaurant—Bistrot Paul Bert.

"Oh my God!" I yelped, my entire body stretching into a smile.

I turned to Dennis and playfully backhanded him in the chest.

"It *is*. Just like you said. Bistrot Paul Bert *is* the best fucking restaurant in Paris!"

Dennis smirk-smiled, his same old self. *Merci, Paris.* Thank you for tolerating us. *À la prochaine*—until next time.

❧ ❧ ❧

The *New York Times* bestselling author of *A Paris Apartment*, *I'll See You in Paris*, and her latest novel, *The Book of Summer*, **Michelle Gable** graduated from The College of William & Mary. After a twenty-year career in finance, she now writes full-time. Michelle lives in Cardiff-by-the-Sea, California, with her husband, two daughters, and one lazy cat.

### Say bonjour:

michellegable.com
Facebook: /MichelleGable
Instagram: @MGableWriter
Pinterest: @MGableWriter
Twitter: @MGableWriter

### The Paris Books:

*A Paris Apartment*
*I'll See You in Paris*

### Favorite Book About Paris:

I have a few favorites, including the ever-popular *The Paris Wife* by Paula McLain, *The Confectioner's Tale* by Laura Madeleine, and the fabulous memoir *We'll Always Have Paris* by Jennifer Coburn.

### Favorite non-Paris travel destination:

I probably shouldn't admit this, but London is my favorite city! It's even a (very small) notch above Paris. For a more relaxing vacation, my choice is

Nantucket, which happens to be the setting of my
third book.

**Strangest must-have travel item:**
I don't have a strange item, other than that I always
bring workout clothes, but I'm an excellent packer.
Two days or two weeks, Paris or London or New
York, I can cram it all into one carry-on.

**In Paris, you can skip . . .**
The Eiffel Tower isn't that exciting, other than when
it's lit up at night, but of course in Paris you have to
see the *Le Tour*!

**In Paris, you must . . .**
I've learned my lesson . . . there is no "must-do"
Paris experience. The only "must" is to find what
works for you, your travel companions, and your
mood. But if I have to name something, I think it's
important to give yourself time to explore whatever
neighborhood you're staying in.

⚜ ⚜ ⚜

# PARIS IS YOUR MISTRESS

*Ellen Sussman*

When my marriage was failing, I barely noticed. I was newly in love with someone else, someone thrilling, sexy, utterly captivating. I was in love with Paris.

My husband and I moved to Paris when I was five months pregnant with our second child; our first daughter was a year and a half old. We had been living in New Jersey, and both of us were yearning for an adventure. Maybe we were yearning for something that our marriage wasn't providing, but we didn't know that yet.

We had been married seven years (itch time?), and I was struggling with a host of problems. I hated suburbia, I was having trouble writing my first novel and even more trouble selling my short stories, and though I loved my baby, I was bored to tears by much of our daily routine. My husband was frustrated by the limitations of his position with the computer company where he worked . . . and worked and worked. No doubt he dreaded coming home to a grumbling wife. I wasn't all too keen about greeting an exhausted, unhappy husband at the end of a very long day.

*Bonjour*, Paris. My husband dreamed up a job in the City of Love and convinced his boss to send us off for a European adventure. I remember our first day in Paris—January 1988, cold, blustery, and astonishing. I felt an onslaught of sensory input—the richest *chocolat chaud* I had ever tasted, the startling sight of the Eiffel Tower piercing the ice-blue sky, the delirious cheers of children watching the marionette show in the Luxembourg Gardens. I had the odd feeling that I was a child, like the one in the stroller I pushed—seeing a world that was thrillingly brand-new.

I needed that jolt to my system. I needed the sound of a new language in my ears (*Voilà! Champignon! Bibliothèque!* What magical words!), the sight of those glamorous French women striding across the street, scarves thrown over their shoulders, legs a mile long wrapped in fishnet stockings. I needed new tastes—crusty *pain Poilâne*, complex Bordeaux wine, pungent cèpes from the farmers' market, briny oysters from Brittany. Even the smells were exotic—a woman beside me on the Métro, awash in a garden of lavender, a cheese shop that exuded earth and rain, a bookseller by the Seine sending wafts of ancient texts and cigar smoke my way.

Here was my first surprise: Every day was just like that first day. I marched through the city with my eyes wide open, my senses on high alert. I don't remember noticing the smell of winter back in New Jersey, or the way children invented games on the merry-go-round, or how a beggar on the subway recited his life story like a poem. Maybe those things happened back home but I was too numb to notice. At thirty-one, I had been leading my life as if I no longer expected the unexpected. I know those people, that food, those buildings, that park, these seasons. In Paris, I knew nothing.

I woke up. I had boundless energy and wanted to roam the streets for hours on end, my daughter bundled into her stroller, the one in my belly somersaulting with her own enthusiastic response. I started to feel as beautiful as those women who strutted across Parisian streets, proclaiming their sexuality with their fierce strides and their skin-hugging clothes.

What was my husband doing all that time? I don't remember. I know he went to work. I know we often went to dinner parties and sometimes went out for dinner together. But that thrill I felt on the street, that riot of sensation, that onslaught of surprise? It wasn't happening in my apartment, around the breakfast table, or, sad to say, in the bedroom. I wasn't paying much attention to the guy from my old life. My new life was outside, en plein air, and life on the streets was a daily (hourly, minute-by-minute) seduction.

I imagine that he, too, was falling in love with Paris. He, too, raved about our exotic home to all our friends and family. He, too, seemed to be in the thrall of a mad crush. Isn't that wonderful? Both of us so happily ensconced in our Parisian life? I had new expat friends who were torn apart by radically differing views of their experience—one adored Paris and the other yearned to be back in the arms of New York City. What a shame, my husband and I told each other, in passing. Aren't we lucky?

I'll take the baby to the museum today! I'll take the two-year-old to the park! *Au revoir! Bisous*—kisses!

A year after we landed in Paris, my husband left his job. Everyone expected us to pack our bags, our babies, and our jaunty berets, and head home. *Mais non!* We're just getting ready! Finally, my French was passable. I learned French along with my daughters—playground French—and though they spoke without an accent, mine was god-awful. The Parisians nonetheless loved my hearty efforts and offered feasts of conversation. I had told a stylist to cut off my hair and now sported a gamine pixie cut. I started to pay attention to style, something this hippie had disavowed for way too long. I bought new clothes for my post-baby body, clothes that wrapped around my curves and made me feel feminine. Seductive.

My husband found some consulting projects and I found a teaching job. We had some savings and we would use that up—anything to stay in Paris. That rush of new love never seemed to wear thin. Perhaps it even deepened as we became more familiar with our city and more adept at all things *parisien*. We discovered the flakiest croissants, the perfect bistro, our girls' favorite park, my most astonishing morning run, the cozy neighborhood jazz club, the long lazy walk along the Seine.

Early on in our stay, we were invited to a wedding. A man asked me to dance and while holding me close, he whispered in French, "I would like to make love with you." I now cringe when I remember what happened next. I cut off the dance and reported him to the hostess. How flattering that he tried to seduce you, she told me. You could politely say no. Or, if you were interested, you might tell him what you would like to do with him. And so began my introduction to the French rules of seduction.

We learned more rules. At a dinner party, spouses are never seated next to each other. Each person is expected to charm his or her tablemate. Flirtation is an art, seduction a higher one. It's a game that everyone can play. Isn't it fun?

I imagine now that many French men and women flirt, feast, and fill themselves with a sexual energy that they then bring home to their partner. If you feel sexy all day, you'll feel sexy at night. But I don't remember feeling sexy when my husband and I returned from those parties. I remember yearning instead for the wicked older gentleman who had whispered dirty words in French—*un petite cours de français, ma cherie*—during a dinner party or the slyly handsome man on the Métro who leaned across the space between our seats and asked me to follow him home.

At some point, about four years into our Parisian love fest, my husband and I realized that our own romance had fizzled. We no longer paid very much attention to each other, and we bickered in a way that we had vowed we never would. When he traveled for business I was secretly glad to have the time alone. When I planned trips back to the States with the girls, he would suddenly find a job that prevented him from joining us. I can't remember how we made the decision to see a couples therapist or where we got her name, but I vividly remember our first visit.

She was French, in her fifties, and spoke English with a heavy accent. Of course she was stylish (those damn scarves—I never learned how to wear one properly) and attractive and listened

to us with a watchful gaze. When we were done telling our stories, she paused for a brief moment.

And then she said, "Paris is your mistress."

There was a kind of delight in the way she spoke those words.
Was she saying: "You're cheating on each other, giving someone
else your love and attention"? Or was she saying: "You've both
been distracted by your passion for Paris, and in the French way,
this has kept your marriage together"?

"We will talk about this next week," she told us. "Our time
is up." (Therapy is therapy, in any language.)

That next week my mother was diagnosed with ovarian cancer and I flew to Miami to be with her. In some cruel twist of fate,
my husband's sister was also diagnosed with a devastating form of
cancer—at the age of twenty-seven. A couple of weeks later, when
I returned to Paris, my husband and I spent another hour with
the couples therapist. She listened to our new stories—of grief, of
impending loss, of the terrible distance between us and our dying
loved ones—and she said, "We will wait for a later time to talk
about your marriage. You have other things on your mind."

I wonder now if that very smart therapist might have helped
us to repair our marriage. We never gave her that chance. We
both spent a very difficult year flying back and forth to the
States, watching our loved ones slowly die. We took turns on
these grim voyages—one of us would stay home with our young
daughters, and the other would sit in the hospital in Miami or
Milwaukee. I don't remember if we fought during that year or if
we ever made love. My mind was elsewhere. Even Paris lost her
luster.

At the end of that year, when both my mother and sweet Shari died, we decided to move back to the States. We felt adrift—rootless with our core families so suddenly altered, too far from our remaining family. So without new jobs or much of a plan, we moved to Palo Alto, California, to begin a new life.

What happens when the affair ends? Paris was gone. And I was left with my husband, both of us grieving, both of us a little lost and terribly lonely. We did not comfort each other. We did not strike out boldly into this new world, hand in hand. We drifted through our new life, looking for new jobs, schools for the girls, doctors, friends. I remember feeling tired, bored, old.

I had been fueled by my affair with Paris for five years, and without that energy, some light went out in me. I'm pretty sure my husband felt the same way. We barely had the energy to fight—we just passed each other by, mumbling to each other: It's your turn to take the girls to school, can you do the food shopping, will you be home tonight?

I kept thinking about that wise therapist's words: *Paris is your mistress.* So now that's she gone, why aren't we falling back in love? Was it too late? Once you've cheated, is the damage done? In the end, I think Paris kept us married for an extra five years. We were so entranced by our mistress that we failed to see what was right in front of our eyes: a failing marriage. And when our mistress went away, we couldn't deny the truth.

And yet it took us five *more* years to end our marriage. Both of us were unhappy, both of us tried to stay together for the sake of the girls. That never works. I remember my older daughter at ten years old writing a short story about a ten-year-old girl waiting for her parents to announce their decision to divorce. We weren't fooling anyone.

Soon after we split up, I tumbled madly, wildly into love. And a funny thing happened: My senses woke up. I was fired with a kind of sizzling energy that reminded me of those early days in France. I found those old sexy Parisian clothes and wrapped my body in them. I burned with desire; I luxuriated in pleasure. It seemed to affect every part of my life. I felt more creative in my work, more compassionate with friends, more patient with my kids. I opened my heart and let love in.

I've now been with the new guy for almost nineteen years. And the lesson I've learned this time around? To keep my eyes wide-open, my senses on high alert. To keep my sexuality alive and pulsing. To treat my guy as if he were my lover, with the same kind of excitement and a frisson of illicit pleasure. We got married fifteen years ago, but my pet name for him is *boyfriend*. His for me? *Girlfriend*. He's the one I'm whispering to at the dinner party; he's the one I follow off the mountain path as we find a place to nestle in the grass.

*Merci*, Paris. You taught me so much about living life fully. You woke me up and kept me on fire for five heady years. You gave me a taste of what I so deserved—a life of passion, a life of wild, crazy desire. Thanks to you, I found it. My second husband and I visit you again and again—we're headed into your arms in a week, in fact. And it will be a *ménage à trois* for us. Because we know what you offer, you saucy flirt. We'll grab it and we'll grab each other and we won't let go.

❧ ❧ ❧

**Ellen Sussman** is the *New York Times* bestselling author of four novels: *A Wedding in Provence, The Paradise Guest House, French Lessons*, and *On a Night Like This*. She is the editor of two critically acclaimed anthologies, *Bad Girls: 26 Writers Misbehave* and *Dirty Words: A Literary Encyclopedia of Sex*. She teaches through Stanford Continuing Studies and in private classes.

### Say bonjour:
ellensussman.com
Facebook: /EllenSussman
Instagram: @EllenSussman
Twitter: @EllenSussman

### The Paris Book:
*French Lessons*

### I write about Paris because . . .
I lived in Paris for five years, from 1988 to 1993. For those years I lived with my eyes wide-open, feasting daily on everything I saw, heard, smelled, tasted, touched. I couldn't wait to write about it, but it took many years before I could find my way in. On a teaching trip to Paris, I bought my husband a week of lessons with a French tutor. She turned out (of course) to be a beautiful woman. What a gift! And so I found my way in—to tell the story of

three Americans who spend one hot summer
day with their French tutors, walking the streets of
Paris.

**Favorite Paris moment:**

When I'm in Paris, I walk and walk and walk. It's
my way of knowing the city, of feeling its energy, of
discovering new favorite parks, cafés, museums.

**Least favorite Paris moment:**

Rainy winters, gray skies.

**Favorite non-Paris travel destination:**

Provence. The summer version of Paris.

**In Paris, you can skip . . .**

The Champs-Élysées. It no longer has anything to
do with the true Paris. It's a shopping mall for
tourists.

**In Paris, you must . . .**

You get a sense of real life while strolling through
the farmers' markets. After you've bought the best
*pain au chocolat* you can find, sit at a café and watch
the Parisians saunter by.

⚜ ⚜ ⚜

# A MYTH, A MUSEUM, AND A MAN

*Susan Vreeland*

Coming out of the Louvre for the first time, I was dizzy with the love of art. It was 1971, and I was twenty-five years old, on a university tour of five European cities. Never had history and art been more vibrant for me, their voices more resonant, their images more gripping. I stood on Pont Neuf on the Île de la Cité and made a pledge to myself that the art of this newly discovered world would be my life's companion.

On this first trip to Europe, my only art background having been watching in awe as my great-grandfather turned daubs of oil paint into a landscape, I felt myself a pilgrim. To me, art museums were imbued with the sacred. Before the Palais du Louvre opened as a museum in 1793, it had been the symbol of the wealth, power, and decadence of the monarchy for six centuries. The transformation from a royal palace to a national museum was a grand cultural gesture, expressing the egalitarian values of the French Revolution. How could I not take advantage of such a sacred public trust?

Painting, sculpture, architecture, music, religious and social history—I was swept away with all of it, wanting to read more, to learn languages, to fill my mind with rich, glorious, long-established culture wrought by human desire, daring, and faith. I wanted to keep a French Gothic cathedral alive in my heart. And I wanted a cordial relationship with French people, one peppered with laughter and lively conversations about art and history over a *café crème* in a sidewalk café.

"*Impossible, Madame,*" I heard at the back of my mind. "The French are snobs, especially Parisians. A cordial relationship? It will never happen."

A barrier rose before me that I longed to vault. But how?

Henry Higgins, the linguistics professor in *My Fair Lady*, asserted, "The French don't care what they do, actually, as long as they pronounce it properly." As for me, I had to take the dangerous plunge with my imperfect, sorely limited French.

Standing on an excursion boat dock, I attempted a simple pleasantry with a Parisian woman wearing a cream-colored Chanel suit with a flirtatious flared skirt. Maybe she would agree that it was a beautiful day, that the Seine and the neo-Renaissance buildings on its banks were impressive. I guessed at *impressif.* After all, the masculine form of "creative" was *creatif.* The masculine of "apprehensive" was *appréhensif.* Also: *agressif, passif, pensif.* Without a word in response, she rolled her eyes beneath her mascara toward her handsome companion and turned her creamy gabardine shoulder in my direction, allowing her peaches-and-cream silk scarf to float in the obliging breeze. Back in my hotel room, I checked my hefty Larousse French-English dictionary: "Impressive, adj.—*impressionnant*." Not *impressif*.

"*Zut!*" That expletive of frustration I had learned from my French teacher burst out. If all the French were indeed as haughty as this woman on the dock, I could look forward to using that expression often.

Not to be outdone, I went down to the reception desk at the hotel to ask for another bath towel—in French. Simple enough. A towel was a *serviette*.

"Speak English," he said brusquely, without looking up from the hotel ledger.

What a put-down. "*Zut!*" I said again, the word exploding onto the shiny, impassive top of his bald head.

"How do you expect me to learn French if you don't let me try to speak it?" I asked. Detecting too much sharpness in my tone, I repeated my towel request in softer French.

One must always be polite to the French, even if the person one is addressing isn't.

I learned that sprinkling one's conversation with *madame, monsieur, s'il vous plaît, merci beaucoup,* and *vous êtes très gentil* was necessary to unlock the hearts of the French. These encounters succeeded in prompting me to take more French language classes in order to break through the barriers of poor pronunciation, improper tense usage, and limited vocabulary.

An embarrassing faux pas early in my trips to France occurred when I asked a bus driver, *"Où est la guerre?"* My intention had been to ask, *"Où est la gare?"*—where is the train station? Inadvertently, I had asked where the war was. Oops.

He wasn't gruff. He wasn't snobbish. He simply brushed me off by saying that he didn't understand me, which I interpreted as a lack of patience with my ignorance. His refusal to try to decipher my mistakes, I came to see, was the result of the tedium of dealing with thousands of linguistically impaired tourists who visit Paris. He shifted the gears on the bus, preparing to leave me at the curb.

I was desperate. "Where do the trains come?" I demanded, in English.

*"Les trains? À la gare, mademoiselle. Gah, ah, ah,"* he stressed, correcting my pronunciation. *"La gare.* Two streets to the left."

I accepted his language lesson with chagrin.

Despite their impatience with my clumsy attempts at their lovely language, I found that Parisians possessed a hidden capacity for kindness.

After a ski mishap in California, I needed to use a cane for a short period of time. Unfortunately, that coincided with another trip to Paris. While waiting with my husband and a friend toward the middle of a queue that snaked around the Musée d'Orsay, a woman wearing a badge came charging toward us from the building, waving her arm toward her chest. *"Venez-vous, s'il vous plaît,"* she said, inviting me to leave the queue and enter the museum with her. I indicated that two other people were with me. She gestured again, including them. Thus she relieved a stranger with a cane from having to stand and wait. Leave it to the French to have such a gracious policy.

The next day, noticing my cane, an elderly man on a bus gave me a seat reserved for the handicapped. He and I carried on a spirited but limited conversation, with smiles, even chuckles, until we arrived at his stop. I couldn't believe it. I was actually sharing mutual chuckles with a Frenchman!

On another trip, I missed a single small step into a courtyard and fell flat, like Goofy, the clumsy companion of Mickey Mouse. Of course, my awkward display just had to occur in front of a busy outdoor café. My husband helped me to my feet, and I rubbed my throbbing knee, unsteady and humiliated. I expected only momentary curiosity from the diners and waiter, and a return to their conversations, maybe even laughter at my stumble. Instead of rolling his eyes at me, the waiter immediately set out a chair, fetched ice wrapped in a dishtowel, brought me an unasked-for (but welcome) *café crème*, offered me an aspirin, and invited me to sit for as long as I wanted, even after the café closed. With trembling dignity, I said in French, "*Merci, monsieur. Vous êtes très gentil*"—you are very kind. His smile was compassionate and sincere when he said he hoped I would feel better soon. I held my husband's arm and hobbled back to the hotel. Unlike the earlier hotel desk clerk who had ordered me to speak English, this more benevolent hotel clerk advised us on where to go for an elastic bandage.

By far, the most superb example of Parisian graciousness came in the form of Monsieur Jean Habert.

It was the famous Impressionist Pierre-Auguste Renoir who brought Monsieur Habert into my life. Though he was born in Limoges in 1841, Renoir was a true Parisian, having spent his childhood living in a slum located in the former guard houses between the twin palaces of the Louvre and the Tuileries. The son of a tailor who was himself the son of a shoemaker, Renoir was reserved, thin, mournful-faced, and plagued by a fear of calling attention to himself. However, he did have the courage to venture into the Louvre frequently as a young lad. For him, his love of paintings trumped timidity. He must have thought that a poor man desiring to be an artist couldn't afford to be shy.

To him, nothing was as joyful as walking slowly through the Louvre, learning from the masters. Later in life, he wrote, "It was like meeting old friends in whom I was always finding new and charming qualities," even daring to touch the work of those old friends if a guard wasn't watching. He longed to express the pleasure of caressing the soft roundness, achieved through color gradations alone, of a young girl's painted cheek, and to run his fingertips over the thick, oily impasto to feel where Rembrandt's brush had left globs of paint protruding from the surface of the canvas.

I shared his yearning, but didn't dare act on it.

In 1860, at nineteen, Renoir registered for a year's pass to copy paintings in the Louvre, a typical art student's practice in the nineteenth century. One painting in particular Renoir returned to again and again, was *Les Noces de Cana* (*The Marriage Feast at Cana*), by Paolo Caliari, *dit* Veronese. The largest painting in the Louvre, measuring 22 feet 3 inches in height by 32 feet in width, it was painted in 1563 for the refectory of the Benedictine monastery on the Venetian island of San Giorgio Maggiore.

The work depicts Jesus performing his first miracle, turning the water into wine before some thirty dinner guests, plus servers and musicians and an additional two dozen onlookers on an upper terrace. But it wasn't the miracle that was important to Renoir. What *was* important to him was the angle of the left arm of the U-shaped table in Veronese's painting. By using this same angle in his 1881 masterpiece *Le déjeuner des canotiers* (*Luncheon of the Boating Party*), Renoir enabled the viewer to see all fourteen of his friends lingering in pleasant conversation after lunch.

Those people seated and standing around Renoir's luncheon table, as the Venetians did in Veronese's painting, became the characters in my 2007 novel of the same name.

In 2004, while in Paris doing research for that novel, I was determined to follow Renoir's example and see the feast table that had inspired him. Arriving with my husband at the Salon Carré on the second floor of the Louvre, we found the door locked. A sign stated that the room was closed for renovation. When I explained to the nearby guard my need to see *The Marriage Feast*, which I considered entirely legitimate since I was close to finishing the first draft, he responded sternly, "*Impossible, madame!*"

I tried it in French. I tried it in English. After two more "*Impossibles*" from two other guards, I approached a guard standing alone, a thin man with sunken cheeks reminiscent of Renoir himself, and pleaded for him to let me in if he watched my every move. It wasn't quite a smile that he gave me. More like a sympathetic flash of amusement at an importunate child. No curt "*Impossible, madame.*" Kindly, he said that I might ask at the information desk in the Pyramid. Even that hint of possibility gave me hope. Not *all* Frenchmen were gruff.

The information desk was semicircular, with half a dozen attendants, and a queue of people in front of each. I chose the attendant with the longest line, thinking she might be more thorough than the others. After explaining the reason for my request, she gave me a slip of paper with a phone number. No name, just a number.

Thus began my battle with the French pay phone system. Which numbers were prefixes, which were necessary for calling from foreign telephones, and what numbers could be dropped were perplexing mysteries meant to keep me from communicating with the French. Why have a number if it must be ignored?

Three days later, after much frustration, I was connected to a receptionist. She transferred my call to a Monsieur Habert. Feeling courageous but nervous, I stumbled through my request in French, which made me feel part of the art world, therefore deserving of some concession. I explained my need to see *The Marriage Feast at Cana*. His response came quickly: "Speak in English, please."

*Zut!* Deflated again.

His second response was also in English: "Meet me on Monday at 14:00. Use the Porte des Lions entrance and speak to the receptionist."

"*Merci, monsieur*," I repeated half a dozen times, gushing my appreciation.

Now, just where was the Porte des Lions? The next morning, my husband asked a passerby on the street, who informed us that it was on the Seine side at the west end of the building. West? Which way was west? I was deplorably naive, but mustered the courage to ask a man waiting at a signal light. Downstream, he answered, with a gesture and even a smile. I checked the river to see which way the water was moving.

I could hardly contain my excitement until Monday. The receptionist just inside the Porte des Lions made a quick phone call and pointed to a narrow elevator. Luckily, there was only one button in the elevator to push. The door slid open, and my husband and I were met by a short, dapper man with round cheeks, wearing a navy blue suit, crisp white shirt, and a red cravat—the living embodiment of the French flag. As he led us through a service corridor, he explained that the Louvre was originally a fortress built in the twelfth century in the center of the growing city of Paris, but that it had been razed in the fourteenth century to make way for a royal palace. François I again ordered its demolition in 1527 to build a larger palace in the Renaissance style. I felt I was following this man through history.

He greeted the guard, opened the door, and there we were, in the Salon Carré, the gallery to which we had been denied entrance before, surrounded by tall ladders, paint cans, and scaffolding, the paintings covered with sheets of plastic. He directed me to the largest, which practically reached the ceiling, climbed the ladder, and swept off the plastic sheet covering the enormous masterpiece that Renoir had studied—all this for someone he didn't know, who had provided no credentials, and who could not speak proper French. This was the cordial relationship with the French that I had longed to experience. Was it my insistence on seeing a specific work of art, perhaps one he loved and imagined I did, too? Was that what set us on friendly terms?

All this before I had a chance to explain my reason for being so intent on seeing this painting—that I was writing a novel about Renoir's *Luncheon of the Boating Party* and that he had consulted the Veronese painting when he was formulating the structure and angle of the two tables in *his* painting.

I wasn't prepared for the enormity of the canvas. I stood enraptured by its intricate composition of a gala feast and the bright Venetian color harmonies, which *monsieur* eagerly pointed out, taking pleasure in telling me the many things to notice.

He spoke of Veronese's masterly freedom of interpretation by transposing the biblical episode to the sumptuous setting of a Venetian wedding. He reveled in the splendor of the costumes—ruby red and emerald green gowns—the jewels entwined in women's coiffures, the sparkling tableware, the animated individuality of the guests, and the classical architecture behind them. It was clear that he was proud of France for owning this masterpiece even though it wasn't by a French painter, and wanted me to appreciate it. How could I not?

I mentioned that the angle of Renoir's table was indeed similar to the left angle of Veronese's U-shaped banquet table. He rubbed his chin, nodded thoughtfully, and admitted that he hadn't known of the similarity. Renoir's painting had been purchased by Duncan Phillips, an American collector, from a Parisian gallery in 1923, and Monsieur Habert had never been to the Phillips Collection in Washington to see it.

In a letter to him I sent him after I returned home, with accompanying research quotes from five sources connecting the two paintings, specifically the left angle of Veronese's table, I wrote, "I appreciated enormously your insightful comments. I learned things I would never have been able to discover other-wise, so in the end, it was good for me that the painting had been inaccessible to me. If it had been on display, I wouldn't have been led to you . . . I must express my heartfelt gratitude for the gift you gave me in that hour."

His response was brief but sincere, thanking me for my re-search and adding, "I didn't realize how much Renoir was in-debted to Veronese for his *Le déjeuner des canotiers*. I am looking forward to reading your book. Best wishes for your novel. Jean Habert."

With those sentences, all my assumptions about French snobbishness vanished.

Two years later, on another research trip, I wanted to see Monsieur Habert again, so I had to think up a reason. It came to me easily. If I were to include in my novel a scene of Renoir visit-ing this painting, where had it been hanging in 1880, the year Renoir painted it? Armed with this question, I wrote to inform him of my impending visit. He responded in a longer letter, this time in French because I had written to him in French, saying that on the dates I would be in Paris he would be taking down a large exhibition, but that he would find time to show me the "*dos-sier historique*" of Veronese's painting. He signed it: Jean Habert, *Conservateur en chef au département des Peintures.*

*Oh là là!* I had no idea that I had been having this conversa-tion with the Louvre's chief curator of paintings, a man of much importance in the world of art. He hadn't even hinted earlier about his high position. My appreciation for French people deepened.

On our next trip, using the same phone number, I tried to

reach Monsieur Habert but couldn't make contact. Our trip was nearly over and I was in despair that I had missed my chance. Then one lovely day when my husband and I were strolling along the Seine, with the Louvre on our right, he had the wild idea of going into the Porte des Lions uninvited.

With my heart pounding like a kettledrum, we asked the receptionist if we could see Monsieur Habert. She made a call, and quickly told us to take the same small elevator right behind us, and there he was, waiting for us, all smiles, with a twinkle in his eyes, as though he was going to reveal a surprise or a secret. I was just happy that he remembered us.

He ushered us into a room of row after row of tall filing cabinets, which must have been the archives. He walked down an aisle between them, informing us that the seventy thousand works of art in the Louvre each had its own dossier. He went right to the desired cabinet, plucked out a fat file, and sat us down at a large, highly polished library table.

"One must read the pages from back to front to understand the history," he said. "In that way, we will find your required information."

He flipped over the folder and turned to the back page, a handwritten acquisition document dated 1798 on yellowed paper, indicating that *Les Noces de Cana* had been plundered from the monastery by Napoleon's troops, cut in half for the journey, and stitched back together in Paris. He didn't seem particularly embarrassed by this proof of its spurious acquisition. He simply translated the page for me without comment.

A few pages later it was revealed that the painting had not been returned in the post-Napoleonic conciliation treaty of 1815, which included restitution of looted artworks. He was similarly unperturbed by this information. He simply announced, "Ah, there you have it. A different feast painting was shipped to Venice instead. So now it's rightfully ours." He glanced sideways at me to make sure I understood France's right to ownership, then under his breath, he added, "Charles Le Brun. We got the better of the deal."

After many more pages recording the art historical studies, the conservation, the cleaning, and the framing, we reached a map of Salon Carré dated 1875, showing the position of this huge painting. Then, another map dated 1885, showed the painting on the same wall.

"You can be fairly sure, Madame, that the painting must have been in that position in 1880, your target year."

I thanked him profusely, well content with our findings, and made a move to leave. He rested his hand on my forearm a moment.

"Let's just see what else we find."

With that all-knowing sparkle in his eye he insisted, kindly, that I stay seated and that we continue through the years. We found that in 1992, the canvas had been spattered by dirty water from a leaking air vent, and when curators were raising the 1.5-ton painting to a higher position on the wall to get it out of harm's way, one of the supports broke, and the painting toppled to the floor. The metal framework tore five holes in the canvas, one of them four feet long. Because he had been so kind to me, I didn't want to ask if that had happened under his watch. Kindness must go two ways.

Finally, we arrived at the front of the folder. I was astonished beyond belief. There, I read that on September 15, 2004, American novelist Susan Vreeland had examined the painting to determine any aspects that Renoir might have used in his *Le déjeuner des canotiers* for inclusion in her novel of the same title—*Luncheon of the Boating Party*.

I may not have been speaking perfect French, but I was in the Louvre! To me, that was the true miracle.

"You knew this was there all along. You put it there, didn't you?"

He grinned his admission and generously invited us to look in other painting dossiers on our own if we wished, and to enjoy the museum for the rest of the day. He was gone in a flash.

In his most recent letter to me, he said that when *Luncheon* was finally exhibited in France at the Musée du Luxembourg, he purchased a large reproduction of it to hang in his home, just like Americans do, just like I had done—which goes to show that the love of art is sufficient to melt stereotypes and create cordial relations.

Certainly there is arrogance and cultural snobbery among the French, but it doesn't take much effort to find their good qualities, too. It was the sage Abraham Lincoln who is famously quoted as saying, "If you look for the evil in man, you will surely find it." The reverse is also true: If you look for the good in man, you will surely find it.

⚜ ⚜ ⚜

A writer of art-related historical fiction, **Susan Vreeland** has written six novels, four of which have been *New York*

*Times* bestsellers: *Girl in Hyacinth Blue*, 1999, featuring an alleged Vermeer painting; *The Passion of Artemisia*, 2002, about Italian Baroque painter Artemisia Gentileschi; *Luncheon of the Boating Party*, 2007, about Pierre Auguste Renoir; and *Clara and Mr. Tiffany*, about the collaboration of artists in glass, Clara Driscoll and Louis Comfort Tiffany, 2011; and in *Lisette's List*, 2014, Pissarro, Cézanne, and Chagall. A collection of stories, *Life Studies*, 2004, features Impressionist painters from the points of view of those who knew them.

### Say bonjour:

susanvreeland.com

Goodreads: Susan Vreeland

### The Paris Books:

*Luncheon of the Boating Party*

*Life Studies*

*Lisette's List*

### Favorite Book about Paris:

*The House I Loved* by Tatiana de Rosnay chronicles the destruction of the old Paris under Baron Haussmann's 1860s plan to make vast renovations, as experienced by one woman who takes a tragic stand against changes that shook Paris to the core. It's rich with details describing the old streets, the shopkeepers and working-class neighbors who must vacate their homes, and gives a tangible flavor of what life was like in the old Paris.

*Favorite song about Paris:*

"*J'ai Deux Amours*" ("I Have Two Loves") by
Josephine Baker, an African-American singer and
dancer wildly popular in Paris cabarets in the 1920s.
This song is featured in *Lisette's List*, and "*La Vie en
Rose*," by Edith Piaf, 1945—so very French.

*Favorite non-Paris travel destination:*

The south of France, London, or Ireland.

*In Paris, you must . . .*

Besides a Seine river cruise, because it shows off
Paris in all its glory, visitors to Paris must see the
Musée de l'Orangerie, which houses *Les Nymphéas*
(*The Water Lilies*), a series of paintings by Claude
Monet. The display consists of two egg-shaped
rooms displaying over 100 linear meters of
waterscape of water lilies, hanging willow branches,
and reflections of trees and clouds creating "the
illusion of an endless whole . . . with no horizon and
no shore," according to Monet. Occupying him for
three decades, it was his gift to the French State,
offered the day after the armistice of November 11,
1918, as a monument to peace.

⚜ ⚜ ⚜

# FRENCH FOR "INTREPID"

*Megan Crane*

All I wanted in my twenties was to be intrepid and free.

Well.

I also wanted a grand and glorious life marked by intellectual richness, a deep and abiding love that was worthy of song and poetry, and perhaps a little dizzying melodrama while I was at it, a satisfying (and objectively awesome) career that was far more than a mere job, a whole lot of money to make sure I could do all the rest, and above all the knowledge unto my very bones that I was doing far more than existing—I was *living*!

Moreover, I really wanted to accomplish all these things with the intrepid spirit I was certain I had. Or so I wrote—extensively—in my journals, all of which I ostentatiously carried around with me lest anyone glance at me and fail to realize I was *made of deep thoughts.*

In truth, I had precious little intrepid spirit. What I had instead was a less than stellar attitude toward the uninspiring entry-level jobs for which I was as unqualified as I was uninterested, and a certain ill-disguised low-level fury that I was stuck in some cubicle rather than off in the world performing marvelous feats of intellectual and physical daring.

Ah, the fruitless outrage of youth.

⚜

I knew what I wanted. The moveable feast. The Paris I'd read about and loved so hard and so deeply in college. Artists and intellectuals cobbled together into sidewalk cafés, living as much on grand ideas as baguettes and strong cigarettes. The Paris of wine and expatriates, Hemingway and Fitzgerald and Stein, uncompromising vision and talk of revolution—or maybe that was *Les Misérables*—and love affairs and fine paintings.

After taking off from this or that city enough times that I should really have bought my own U-Haul to defray the inevitable moving expenses, it was undeniable that I was less the badass rolling stone I imagined myself, unable to suffer a hint of moss as I moved ever closer to my life of mystery and wonder, and more someone who simply ran away when things got predictable.

The trouble with running away, it would not occur to me for years, was that no matter what place or which people I left behind in a cloud of dust when I decided it was time to go, I took *me* right along with my boxes upon boxes of (very heavy) books. And I really didn't like thinking of myself as someone who ran away from things rather than facing the harder work of actually belonging somewhere, despite the fact that I did it again and again. Right about the time I'd figured out my favorite route to whatever dead-end job I was working, a place to get my shoes repaired, and the best pizza delivery, I was already looking for a new place to live, a new city to explore, new people to meet. New, new, new, so I couldn't waste any time getting sick of the same old me.

I can't remember why I decided the cure for running away wasn't to settle down somewhere, but to travel. I was in graduate school by this point, and at some point during the brutal slog toward my dissertation I decided that the only way to survive was to become *a seasoned traveler.*

Once I settled on this, I became obsessed with it. Moving all over the place for no particular reason suggested things about a person's psychology, I'd found. The truth is, most people stay pretty rooted. Moving all over the place on a whim instead of, say, for a job or a partner tended to unnerve people.

*Travel,* by contrast, was universally held to be a good thing. It was broadening! Educational! It would leave me richer no matter the money I spent on it! Everybody said so. I bought novelty postcards of foreign cities and taped them into my journals, where I would then wax rhapsodic about all the places I would go.

I had very specific ideas about what *travel* meant. It meant strolls through gray and giddy London, sophisticated and more than a little posh. It meant little black dresses in sidewalk cafés. Art in graceful museums famous enough to be known the world over and long drives in the Tuscan countryside with a fetching scarf tied *just so* around my hair—which in my fantasies was always a cunning shade of Titian rather than my natural dull brown. Travel meant staying in a nice hotel room and eating in fine restaurants. It meant an easy roller bag, not, say, a backpack that required lugging while drenched in sweat. It was reading an interesting book in a busy café while dressed like Audrey Hepburn. It meant Paris in the springtime, just like the song . . .

Sign me up for travel, please.

❧

I arrived in Paris on a chilly fall day, having swept in on the Eurostar from London. This high-speed train experience whisked me beneath the English Channel, which I'd expected to find marvelous beyond the telling of it, but was, really, just a tunnel—only delightful in retrospect, when looking at a map with all that water.

I didn't let this inauspicious beginning get me down. A good friend of mine was living in London at the time and she and her husband had recommended a specific hotel to me, so once I arrived in the Gare du Nord in Paris I set off to find it. The fact that I didn't speak a word of French (besides the usual inappropriate song lyrics, which were the only thing in my head for my first few hours in Paris) didn't get in my way.

By which I mean I brandished the address of the place in my taxi driver's face and hoped for the best.

The hotel was in a nice part of the city, or nice-adjacent, and the taxi driver was unable to take me to the door. He couldn't tell me why—not even in song lyrics. But I discovered why soon enough when I tried to find the place on foot. The front door of the (probably very cute, in retrospect) boutique hotel was down a very long alleyway. During my late-afternoon arrival, it was gloomy. I rolled my bag over the stones, making a terrific racket, and was soon in my little room featuring a view of at least one Parisian rooftop—but only if I stood on the bed. What I wanted to do was lie on that bed and try to recover from my arrogant assumption that not speaking the language would not be a problem or that doing something that scared me would make me less scared while I was doing it. Possibly in the fetal position.

But I wasn't in Paris—and off on my own solo adventure—to feel sorry for myself. I had too many things to see! And feel! And experience! And more to the point, I was hungry. Not just for food. I was hungry to become the sort of woman who could take solo trips to places like Paris and *thrive.*

I was fairly certain my life hinged on becoming that woman immediately. So, no pressure.

I marched myself out into the city as the autumn night soaked its way down from the gloomy clouds into the ancient streets. It was wetter and colder by the moment, but that didn't bother me. Or rather, I ignored it as I tried to acclimate myself to my new identity of Intrepid Solo Traveler. Doesn't that sound great? In actuality, what was happening was I was having a panic attack, out there all alone in a huge, mysterious city filled with desperately chic strangers and signs I couldn't read unless I stood before them for ten minutes, basically broadcasting the fact that I was a lost tourist to the whole of France.

It was a serious panic attack, and it didn't get better.

No one in the whole world knew where I was at that very minute. No one knew who I was when I found a restaurant and sat there to have dinner with myself and my thoughts, in the middle of a city I'd always wanted to make mine but that, clearly, could take me or leave me. And no one knew who I was when I walked in my very loud, high-heeled shoes down the oppressively dark alley toward the door of my hotel. The very long, very isolated alley that made me break out into a sweat as I hurtled down it, convinced I was about to be jumped at any moment as my shoes broadcast my lonely location.

My friend had stayed there, yes. With her very tall and intimidating husband. I'm sure that to her, that alley was picturesque. To me, it was a nightmare piled on top of a panic attack and a crippling sense of loneliness to boot.

I'll be honest. I did not enjoy my first night in Paris. I slept fitfully, wondering if I should just get on the next train back to London, where, at the very least, if I was jumped in a dark alley, I would understand what was being said to me by my attackers.

At 2:31 A.M. in my tiny Parisian hotel room, where I may or may not have gotten up to pack in a frenzy of sleeplessness, this seemed like an upgrade.

But the night ended the way dark nights always do, and I decided that maybe one fall evening and an alarming alley weren't enough to erase the entire magical history of Paris in my head. Not to mention, it was going to be hard to think of myself as intrepid if I went down—or home—without a fight.

Did I want to be the person who went all the way to Paris for a moveable feast and then ran off home without so much as a nibble? I did not. In fact, it was that thought that got me out of my bed and back down that damned torturous alley, out into a crisp and clear fall day.

*Bring on Paris*, I thought. Maybe a little grimly.

⚜

I had no plan. I had nothing but time and Paris and a great deal to prove to myself about who I really was. So this is what I did: I walked. I wandered wherever the mood took me. I went to the Eiffel Tower and I wandered down the Champs-Élysées until I found myself in the Tuileries Gardens. I spent hours in the Musée d'Orsay and felt as if I could fall straight through the canvas into a Van Gogh and live there forever, surrounded by all that remarkably bright color. I lusted over Rodins and explored the Louvre. I walked down famous streets, I peered in the windows of renowned stores, and I found myself in neighborhoods I'd only ever read about before.

I don't know if I felt intrepid. But the longer I let the city seep into me, the more I felt alive in a way that had nothing to do with books or dissertation chapters or even my own deep panic.

I started to ask myself, what if what I was calling panic was actually just life? What if this was what it felt like when I was actually out living it, not locking myself away in rooms with books or determinedly moving from this city to that to avoid ever really letting myself live a real life in any one of them?

What if I leaned straight into that panic and found out what was fueling it? What if I accepted that feeling for what it was as it happened—not analyzed, not interpreted, not imagined, but raw and real?

It had never occurred to me that a life of mystery and wonder might feel a bit unsettling as it happened, what with all the confusion inherent in both. Just as it had never really crossed my mind that Hemingway's jolly reminiscences about the creative splendor of poverty might have felt a bit less entertaining in the actual moments he and his friends were broke and hungry.

Maybe if it frightened me a little, I was doing it right.

And then, finally, when I'd surrendered myself to the actual experience I was having rather than the one I'd been carrying around in my head for years, I wandered my way into the Left Bank and found what I'd been looking for all that time. Waiting for me just as I'd imagined it. I sat in a famous café I never thought I'd see in person, but had dreamed about for years. I drank strong coffee at an outside table and I watched Paris walk by me in the crisp fall air.

It took me a while to define the unfamiliar feeling inside. Because I was content. As content as I'd ever been. As if the point of all my wandering and dreams of an intrepid life was that sweet, deep quiet down there inside of me, at last.

As if I was whole already, just as I was. No feats of daring required.

Later, I sat on a bench near Notre-Dame as the night fell over the city, dark and thick. The great old cathedral was lit up behind me and Paris was spread out before me, as if it was one more glorious, famous painting. I wasn't afraid anymore. I wasn't in a panic. On the contrary, I felt marvelously alive—delightful and contradictory, confusing and content at once. I didn't care if my soul was marked. I didn't care if the life I was living looked large to others' eyes. I didn't even care if my shoes were loud and announced me to all the strangers around me enjoying the same sweet night, not when they'd helped me discover my own path through this complicated and beautiful place and brought me so much closer to myself.

I'd bought a baguette and some hard cheese and I sat out there in the gathering dark of my new favorite city, making my own little feast at last. No one I knew, out there in the world, had any idea where I was in that moment. No one walking by knew who I was. I could be anything. I could be anyone.

I could finally be me.

That was what Paris did for me, one long-ago weekend on my own. It scared me, then it challenged me. And then it set me free.

⚜ ⚜ ⚜

*USA Today*–bestselling, RITA-nominated, and critically acclaimed author **Megan Crane** has written more than sixty books since her debut in 2004. She's won fans with her women's fiction, chick lit, and work-for-hire young adult novels as well as with the Harlequin Presents titles she writes as Caitlin Crews. If she's not at her desk in the beautiful Pacific Northwest, she's probably out hiking.

**Say bonjour:**
megancrane.com
Facebook: /MeganCraneAndCaitlinCrews
Instagram: @MeganMCrane

**The Paris Books:**
*Majesty, Mistress . . . Missing Heir*
*No More Sweet Surrender*
*Expecting a Royal Scandal*
(all by Caitlin Crews)

**Favorite Paris moment:**
I once spent a long afternoon in the Musée d'Orsay
with my mother and a whole lot of Van Gogh. It was
life-altering as much because of the masterpieces
littered about everywhere as for the conversations
my mother and I had about them.

**Song that reminds you of Paris:**
"Paris" by Carina Round. It's a great song, but also,
it was on a mix I listened to when I was there. It
reminds me of walking through the shadows of a fall
evening down the Champs-Élysées.

**Favorite non-Paris travel destination:**
This changes often, but currently? Iceland.

**Strangest must-have travel item:**
Matilda the traveling wombat. Don't ask.

⚜ ⚜ ⚜

# PARIS, LOST AND FOUND

*Paula McLain*

When I first visited Paris in the summer of 2010, I didn't get anywhere near the Eiffel Tower or Versailles. I didn't stroll goggle-eyed down the Champs-Élysées toward the Arc de Triomphe, or see Monet's famed gardens, or enter a single museum. The Paris I came to see was invisible to most tourists. Replete with monuments, yes, but utterly specific and deeply intimate ones.

I had just finished writing *The Paris Wife*, a novel about Ernest Hemingway and his first wife, Hadley, set in one of Paris's most glorious and romantic time periods, the early 1920s. It was my first historical project, and a book that blew into my life with great force, hijacking my imagination and pinning me—quite literally—to a chair in a Starbucks in Cleveland for the better part of a year between 2008 and 2009, while I channeled Hadley's voice and consciousness, following her down the rabbit hole and out again, into Gertrude Stein's salon, say, where she was having a conversation with Alice B. Toklas. Or into her dim one-bedroom apartment in the Latin Quarter—both places I knew intimately, if only in my mind.

In the best of all possible worlds, I would have traveled to Paris to research the book properly, but my actual world was a hot mess. My children were two, four, and fifteen then. My marriage was incredibly rocky, and the wolf was most definitely on my block, if not yet huffing perilously at the door. I could barely get a shower some days, let alone catapult myself across the Atlantic. But I could read. I got my hands on every possible book I could find . . . on Jazz Age Paris, on Hadley, Ernest, their golden circle of expats. There was bullfighting to learn about, and Alpine skiing, and Modernism. I needed to read all of Hemingway's stories, particularly the early ones, and *The Sun Also Rises*, which I'd *had* to read in high school, but was actually paying attention to this time.

The more I stuffed my brain full of Jazz Age Paris, the stronger I felt the pull of the world and the story, until I felt I might actually die if I didn't spit this book *out* immediately. So I quit the two part-time teaching jobs I had, borrowed money from my in-laws to buy more child care, and parked myself in Starbucks Monday through Friday, writing desperately, passionately, as if my life depended on it. It's entirely possible it did.

But here's the thing. No one ever warns you about the mental health hazards of armchair travel. By the time the book was written, revised, edited, re-revised, and page-proofed, I was so invested in and hooked so hard on the Paris I had built, day by day, word by word, that I wasn't sure I was up to traveling to the actual place. How could it possibly hold up? And if I couldn't find the city as it was then, wouldn't that feel worse than never having gone? Wasn't I just going to get my heart smashed to bits?

The risks were obvious but the idea of not going felt cowardly and backward. I had to go. I had to.

It was raining when I landed at Charles de Gaulle, and still raining when I came out of the Métro station in Paris near the Jardin du Luxembourg, delirious with jet lag, my legs like pancakes. I walked in circles for an hour trying to find my hotel, turning the map over and over in my hands, as if that would make anything clearer. Before long, my luggage was drenched, ditto my shoes, my hair. My glasses were spattered to near uselessness, but I recognized a street when I stumbled onto it. My hotel was still MIA, but just there, just half a block away, was 74 Cardinal Lemoine, the address of Ernest and Hadley's first apartment in Paris.

I'm not sure I can adequately describe the complex emotional cocktail of that moment: joy, relief, gratitude, and astonishment, all blended and addled and heightened by brain fog. The door was bright blue with an iron grille at eye level in the same blue, and chips and scuffs everywhere . . . a lived-in door. Real as anything. I touched the peeling jamb again and again, like someone who'd gone temporarily blind, blinking up at the windows, which were *their* windows, and feeling as if time had been rolled back—just for that moment, just for me; that the past was now, here . . . glinting and sparking palpably. Still golden after all.

I had a fancy digital camera I'd purchased for the trip. I pulled it out of my dripping knapsack, and stopped someone who looked friendly, not even trying to speak the smattering of tourist's French I'd pried from the guidebook. It wasn't a great shot of me, but as I looked at it through the preview screen a few moments later, I felt elated and strangely powerful. *Yes, you were really here*, the photo attested, and always would. *You were, and they were, too, and this is your evidence.* It was as if I'd caught and held the rarest of butterflies in the cage of my hands. The Lost Generation, not so lost after all.

For the rest of that day and the next, I sought out every vestige of Ernest and Hadley's Paris. Here was the zigzagging, cobblestoned rue Mouffetard with the fruit and bread mongers, the tiny strawberries in their wooden baskets—a moveable feast in every sense. The Luxembourg Gardens where Ernest paced like a half-tamed panther after a day's writing, shaggy-haired, hungry, a hole in his shoe. All the good cafés, the Dôme, the Select, Les Deux Magots, Brasserie Lipp, the Closerie des Lilas . . . but not the Ritz, for the Ritz was later, another version of Hemingway, when he had another wife and an entirely different reputation and was no longer happy and poor, borrowing books from Shakespeare and Company.

And there was Shakespeare and Company itself, and Ernest's tiny fourth-floor walkup studio on the rue Descartes, and Gertrude Stein's salon on the quietly elegant rue de Fleurus. There was Ezra Pound's loft, the courtyard to which was hung with a white rose trellis, beaded with rain. If someone had happened along and seen me, camera shaking in my hands, in front of the wrought-iron gate, they might have thought me crazy, crying because I had just spotted the skylight that Hemingway described in his writing. A skylight had me unhinged? Maybe I *was* a lunatic, but I couldn't stop.

These captured images felt imperative, like manifest stamps on my spiritual passport as I walked and walked, my feet tracing the past's footprints, every stop a way of touching and acknowledging the cost of artistry, the losses, what Ernest's books had given him and taken away, what mine had, too, and Hadley's role in both of our lives. In a way, I identified deeply with both of them. And loved both of them, terribly flawed as they both were, she too passive and self-subsuming, and in denial about the way his ambition was coming along to devour them both.

But while their love still flourished, they lived at rue Notre-Dame-des-Champs, the sawmill apartment, as Hemingway always called it, their second home in Paris. The street curves just behind the bustling boulevard Montparnasse, but seems far enough away to feel like another world. The Closerie des Lilas, his unofficial office during these years, was only a few hundred steps away, beyond a high lilac hedge. The marble tables, the white demitasse cups and white saucers, the *café crème*, the sentences in the blue *cahier* notebooks coming smoothly or roughly, or sometimes not at all.

The sawmill apartment had been gone for decades by the time I arrived, but I walked slowly along the street anyway, looking for the bakery Ernest used to cut through to reach Montparnasse. It wasn't hard to locate, exhaling as it did the aroma of warm brioche and croissant and *pain au chocolat*, smells that sent bullets of pleasure into my amygdala. Of course I had to cut through the bakery, too, and as I did, I paused at the door to the basement that said, on a roughly painted sign, "Artistes." This is where Hadley went to play a borrowed piano, I remembered, and I felt a flash of recognition and connection to her life. She was here, exactly here, taking the narrow steps, while their son, Bumby, napped at home or in a pram in the Luxembourg Gardens with Marie Cocotte, their *femme de ménage.*

With goose bumps up my arms, I crouched to snap the photo, and before I knew what was happening, I'd slipped on the rain-damp step, crashing awkwardly, jarringly, onto my tail-bone. The camera fell hard to the pavement and cracked open. Just like that, in one instant, my captured memories were gone, escaped, loosed from their net.

When I finally stopped crying, my problem-solving self stepped in. Surely there was a camera shop somewhere that would sell me a replacement. It wasn't easy to find the store, nor was it easy to discern the cameras' different features when everything was in French, which I couldn't navigate under the best of circumstances. I stood there, looking at the wall of expensive options, counting my remaining euros on my fingers, hating myself and wishing I could go back and do the moment over, being careful. But that was impossible. What was done was done. Telling myself I could write it off as a business expense, I bought the same camera as before. Then, with just a single day left before I headed south from Paris toward Spain and the Côte d'Azur, the next stops on my Hemingway pilgrimage, I retraced my steps, more quickly this time. I barely had to look at the map to orient myself and find the locations again, I realized. For at least in this small slice of Paris, I was no longer just a tourist. I knew exactly where I was.

By the time I reached my train the next afternoon, I had

everything in the can, so to speak. The next stop was San Sebastián, in Basque country, a special place for Hadley and Ernest and one of the most beautiful cities I had ever seen. My dearest friend, Pam, arrived shortly after I did, having flown from Minneapolis to Bilbao to spend part of this trip with me. She'd barely stashed her luggage when I snapped her photo in front of the hotel, or tried to. My camera—the new one—flashed an ominous "error" sign when I tried to view the shot. Panicked, I ran the thing to a camera store, Pam in tow, where I was told, in broken English, that the memory card appeared to be empty. All the Paris photos, the painstaking retakes, were missing. Again.

This time, there were no tears, just a punch-in-the-gut feeling as reality sunk it. The wasted effort, and the loss. I had no evidence of my time in Paris, all those steps, that interfacing, that pilgrimage. Pam and I decided to get drunk, and all of San Sebastián seemed to collude to join us. The World Cup was happening, and Spain was playing well. That night, the streets were deep with bodies, the liquor poured freely, and everyone sang. And sang. And sang. At four o'clock in the morning, the party was still going strong, like Mardi Gras on crack. I lay in my narrow bed looking up at the ceiling, unable to sleep, wondering if the universe was sending me a message with this camera nonsense. Something about evanescence. About how everything, everything flares in front of us and passes away again, like the bursts of song floating up from the street. Here and gone, like breath. For the having, yes, but never for the keeping?

Whatever the message, or even if there was no message, for the rest of the trip I decided to get some Zen on board and surrender a little. And it was magical. For a while. We traveled to Pamplona by bus, back to San Sebastián, then to Biarritz, where we rented a microscopic Fiat that rattled us across the top of the Pyrenees toward Antibes. The trip went seamlessly until it started to rain again, the storm building to near-biblical torrents. At one point near Marseilles, the car lost traction with the road and spun, hydroplaning toward the guardrail. I reached and grabbed Pam's leg in slow motion as we careened sideways, water sheeting up over the hood. We didn't say anything. I'm not sure either of us breathed. When the car finally stalled, stuck to the road again, we were somehow, impossibly, unharmed. We looked at each other, eyes wide, realizing already that this would forever be the night we did not die in a Fiat in the South of France. We wouldn't need a photograph to remember it, though we could definitely use several bottles of wine, or maybe some absinthe, when we reached our hotel, to forget it.

When Pam and I finally parted several days later, I gave her the camera with its new memory card. My luggage was stuffed to the gills, and I was heading straight to Charles de Gaulle on the TGV to catch my flight home. But the rain. Oh, the rain. So much water over the past weeks had damaged the tracks and slowed everything down. The trip, which should have taken six hours, took close to nine. I missed my flight by a mile, and quickly learned that bureaucracy, fare restrictions, and fate had determined that the next flight was two days in the future.

Two days. There were more tears, and then I reached for my credit card and made my way to the shockingly expensive airport

Novotel, too defeated to try to find a hotel in Paris. That night, I ate a wilted Caesar salad in a plastic cup that cost 13 euros, homesick, guilty, missing my children, and feeling absolutely beaten by travel.

The next morning, the sun was shining and I had the whole day. What would I do? What do you think I did? I went to the camera store! I did. And yes, I bought the same model again, and yes, I walked each of the same steps again. And yes, this memory makes me cringe now, at how driven I was to make this particular stand.

It also makes me smile. My time in Paris was like no one else's ever. The ecstasy, the agony, all mine. And as I look at the photos, still . . . hundreds and hundreds of them . . . I know they're not alive, and that they do not suffice. I didn't stop time, or shore up loss, or hold anything at all but my own lopsided journey, jinxed and precious, luckless and singular, fleeting and durable, worth any price.

❧ ❧ ❧

**Paula McLain** is the *New York Times* and international bestselling author of *The Paris Wife* and *Circling the Sun*. She lives in Cleveland with her family.

*Say bonjour:*
    paulamclain.com
    Facebook: /PaulaMcLainauthor
    Instagram: @Paula_McLain

*The Paris Book:*
   *The Paris Wife*

*Favorite Paris moment:*
   I had one of the most memorable meals of my life at Closerie des Lilas, one of Hemingway's favorite cafés, celebrating the birthday of a dear friend. Oh, and the best gin and tonic! It came with its own little ice bucket and silver stir stick. Divine!

*Least favorite Paris moment:*
   On one trip to Paris with my oldest son and a friend, we were all so jet-lagged and essentially brain-dead that it took us nearly an hour to figure out how to open the door of the apartment we'd rented. It came with several keys and a very elaborate system of turns, but in the end, we couldn't open it because we were pulling on instead of pushing the door! Ultimately my son gave up and leaned on the door in frustration, and *voilà*!

*Favorite quote about Paris:*
   "But Paris was a very old city and we were young and nothing was simple there, not even poverty, nor sudden money, nor the moonlight, nor right and wrong nor the breathing of someone who lay beside you in the moonlight."—Ernest Hemingway, *A Moveable Feast*

*Song that reminds you of Paris:*
"Set Fire to the Rain," by Adele . . . because one Thanksgiving some dear friends and I cooked braised rabbit instead of turkey in an amazing VRBO rental in the 6th arrondissement, and had a particularly dramatic lip-sync battle to this song.

*Favorite non-Paris travel destination:*
Kenya.

*Strangest must-have travel item:*
Books. Physical books, and more of them than is remotely sensible. I feel like a Sherpa hauling them around airports, and yet I can't stop.

⚜ ⚜ ⚜

# FAILING AT PARIS

*Eleanor Brown*

Whenever someone asks me how I liked Paris, I feel like I have to lie.

To be fair, the question never comes like that. No one says, "How did you like Paris?" with the same sort of idle disinterest they might ask, "How was Akron?" or "What did you think of Poughkeepsie?"

No, people get very excited about Paris. "Did you love it?" they ask, already preparing the next rush of questions. "Was it amazing?"

These questions have only one acceptable response: "Yes!" delivered at the approximate pitch and excitement level of a boy-band fan.

But this, you see, is a lie.

When I was researching my second novel, *The Light of Paris*, my sweetie and I spent a little over a month in the City of Light. We rented an apartment. We drank coffee in cafés and walked along the Seine and smelled the flowers in the Luxembourg Gardens, and saw enough Impressionist paintings to wallpaper a college dorm room.

See, there you go already. Here is what you're thinking right now: *Did you love it?*

Well, no. I didn't.

I didn't love Paris. I didn't, most days, even like it.

What is *wrong* with me?

I mean, honestly. People have written songs about Paris. When I was looking for a title for *The Light of Paris*, I went to the Wikipedia entry listing songs about Paris. Do you know how many are listed there? Over a thousand! Over a thousand people have gone to the trouble of writing, recording, and releasing songs about Paris, and me? I tried to write one, but there was only one note: *meh*.

It wasn't always that way. When I was a teenager, I took a trip with some friends that involved a daylong layover in Paris. The airline had given us a hotel room for the day, but instead of resting, we headed out, giddy and jet-lag drunk, into the city. We went to the Louvre and saw the Mona Lisa. We rode the Métro, where we befriended a young Italian woman who gave us directions (in English). We ate ham sandwiches on baguettes, which, much to our adolescent American confusion, were spread with butter rather than mayonnaise.

For years, that was my only experience with the city, and it was a pretty good one. Eight hours or so in any city is a good amount of time to fall in love with it without encountering any of its downsides.

Fast-forward to a few years ago. I was visiting my parents, and I can't remember how the subject of Jazz Age Paris arose—but my father told me, quite casually, "Your grandmother lived in Paris for a while, you know. Around 1924."

I most certainly did not know this. To be fair, I hadn't known my grandmother well at all. She was in her seventies when I was born, and then by the time I was old enough to really connect with her, she had already slipped into the cruel grip of Alzheimer's and whoever she had once been was disappearing quickly.

"I'm sorry," I said. "*The* Paris? *The* 1924? Like, F. Scott Fitzgerald Paris? Gertrude Stein Paris? Like, *A Moveable Feast* Paris?"

"*Oui*," my father said.

Okay, he didn't actually say that. I think he just said yes.

But they weren't done. Because then my mother chimed in, equally offhandedly, "And we have all the letters she wrote home while she was there."

ARE YOU KIDDING ME?

As someone interested in family history, this was a delight to hear. As a writer? Well, let's just say when I headed home a few days later, I carried onto the plane a box full of my grandmother's letters, starting in her high school years and, yes, including Paris. I didn't dare check the box as baggage—the contents were literally irreplaceable.

My grandmother's letters are a complete joy, a reminder of how history obscures the lives of ordinary individuals in favor of the more "important" stories of politics, of populations, of trends. Save for a few pieces of slang, I could have written those letters myself—they are filled with her high school agonies over grades and dresses, her college dates and worries about the future, her endless conflicts with her parents, her search for herself.

My grandmother graduated from college in 1922, and spent a year teaching at what sounds a great deal like a reform school for girls before heading off to Europe on a sort of Grand Tour, that finishing rite of passage for men and then women of a certain age and, more important, a certain means.

With a friend, she sailed to England and, after a few weeks there, headed to Paris. From there, they had planned to set off for Italy, but after only a few days in Paris, she had already decided to stay and had begun interviewing for jobs in order to support herself. In 1923, for a woman of her social class, this was a seismic decision, and her letters to her family are clearly attempts to convince them of her maturity and ability to support herself.

I don't have her parents' responses to her letters, but you can infer their disapproval from her increasingly firm insistence that she is going to stay. At the same time, reading her talk about how mature she has become invites a sort of "Oh, *honey*" response. She was twenty-three when she went, and oh boy is she ever twenty-three on those pages. She knows absolutely everything and has no fear about expressing her opinions. Napoleon's tomb? Overdone and gauche.* English women? Frightfully frumpy. Her parents' plan to send her sister to a school she doesn't like? Cruel. The thought of dating the son of a family friend? Ghastly.

She is similarly impassioned about Paris. My grandmother's letters are filled with exaltations about the city's charms.

* *She is not wrong about this.*

"Jean to-morrow night and Bill Sunday—*c'est la vie de Paris!*"

"Lunched at Prunier's yesterday off caviar and lobster. You could have heard me purr for miles. I take to luxury so very easily."

"Heaven only knows what happens to the time in Paris."

"The very streets of Paris thrill me—and I'm *so* glad to be here."

She lived in Paris for a little under a year, but while she was there, she sucked the marrow out of the city. She was young, and Paris was the place to be young, a vibrant city with all the dizzy energy of the 1920s, alive with painters and writers and musicians and every daring and beautiful thing they were creating. Since she was writing to her parents, she occasionally glosses over the more interesting details, but she is still surprisingly honest— she records her dates with both American and French men, describes the cafés and bars she visits, admits staying out dancing all night only to stagger in to work in the morning. (At one point she sends them a photo of herself, sadly lost to time, in which she describes herself as looking "like the back end of a night at the bar," and it's entirely possible that's when it was taken.)

If you read enough about Jazz Age Paris, it's hard not to want to be there yourself, and my grandmother's letters had that very effect on me. As I read them, I began to put together a story about a young woman heading to Paris, breaking her family's rules and her own expectations of herself to forge the life she wanted to live, at just the time in history when that began to be genuinely possible for so many women. But I wanted to be able to write that story with authority, since Paris as a *place* is such a vital part of what became the story of Margie in *The Light of Paris*.

And so I set off to follow in my grandmother's footsteps, to research her story in order to create my own.

For research purposes, I was determined to follow the exact route my grandmother had taken. And so we sailed from New York City to Southampton, England, which is more fun than it sounds, then took a train to London and then Dover, which is about as much fun as it sounds, and finally a ferry to Calais and another train to Paris, which is less fun than it sounds, mostly because we were very, very tired by then.

The idea of traveling *à la* 1923 sounds very romantic, but I am going to tell you, from painful experience, that no matter how much the TSA stinks, it does not stink half as much as turning what could be ten hours of travel into ten very long days.

But we did finally arrive, and I began my quest to experience Paris as my grandmother had. I'd made a list of all the places she had mentioned visiting—from the American Library, where she'd worked, to the gardens of the Rodin museum, where she'd somehow wrangled a private tour, to the cafés so popular with the artists and expats of 1920s Paris—and I set about visiting them. Every day, I woke up, planned where I would go, saddled up with my camera and my notebook, and went out to experience the city.

There were only a few problems with my plan.

First of all, while you can go to Paris, you can't go to Paris in 1924. My grandmother's Paris was not the Paris I was in. Nearly a century separated those cities, to begin with, with all the attendant modernization, for better or for worse.

Second, I was not my grandmother. When she went to Paris, she was in her early twenties, and a charmingly naive, girlish twenty-something at that. She had all the wide-eyed innocence that makes one's first trip abroad such a delicious thing, and she was breaking free of her traditional, coddling family. I was a rather more time-worn near-forty, of the age where the only thing we have to run from is the grim reality that despite our best efforts, we have turned into our parents.

And then, of course, there was Paris.

I was okay in Paris for about a week. And then, little by little, I started to realize I wasn't happy there. The buildings were pretty, but the architectural standardization inflicted upon the city by Baron Haussmann also makes large swaths of it look disappointingly similar.

The food was fine. Just fine.

The Parisians were not rude, as advertised, but nor were they particularly charming (though boy howdy, are they a people who know how to wear a scarf). And everywhere was crowded, so crowded. The museums were so crowded you couldn't see the art. The cafés were so crowded you were pressed up against your neighbors' elbows. Smoking had been banned indoors, so all the smokers ate at the adorable tables on the sidewalks while the nonsmokers huddled inside.

It wasn't terrible. It was . . . just a city.

Paris is incredibly popular in Japan, so much so that some Japanese tourists to the city have been known to develop a psychiatric disorder known as Paris Syndrome, involving physical symptoms such as dizziness and sweating, and psychological ones including hallucinations, paranoia, and depression.

*Ooh là là!*

Reasons cited for the disorder include extreme culture shock and exhaustion, but the root cause seems to be a dramatic difference between the idealized image of Paris presented in Japanese media and the reality of the city. These tourists, articles claim, arrive expecting streets full of Parisians clad in Chanel, slim and chic, the city's famous buildings gleaming in the sunlight. What they discover is that despite all Paris's beauty, it has the problems of any large city, coupled with a French flair they find uncomfortable. Parisians, for instance, litter the City of Love with more than 350 tons of cigarette butts per year, according to the *Guardian*. Pickpockets abound, paying special attention to tourists, especially those traveling in groups, making them easily identifiable. The buildings are indeed lovely, but they can wear the stain of Paris's overwhelming smog—in 2015, the smog was so terrible that Paris briefly won the dubious honor of having the worst air quality in the world.

And the people . . . well, the people, as Eddie Izzard says, "are kind of fucking *French* at times."

Paris can literally drive you crazy.

Or not. Maybe Paris isn't the problem. Maybe, as with Paris Syndrome, it's us and our expectations of it. Maybe it wasn't Paris at all. Maybe it was me.

I am technically the youngest child, which by all rights should mean I'm the sort of easygoing free spirit I wrote about in *The Weird Sisters*. But my sisters are quite a few years older than I am, which also means I've got more than a bit of only child in me. And a lifetime of experiences has also given me what I am going to generously term "control issues."

I had a plan, Paris. I had a list of things to accomplish. I had places to go and people to see. I had an idea of the way things Ought to Be. And you kept getting in the way.

Probably the most important problem of our trip was our failure to pack the correct footwear. I had brought two pairs of shoes—a new and alarmingly expensive pair of comfort sandals, which I had worn only around the house, and a thin-soled pair of sneakers, which I wore regularly at home, finding them much more "natural" than a heavier, padded pair of sensible walking shoes (I am sure you can see where this is going). The first day I wore the sandals, I strained my Achilles tendon while stepping off the bus in front of the Louvre, and I wore them rarely afterward, as they had a tendency to set off that pain again. As for those minimalist sneakers, well, let's just say they were the first indication that Paris had no interest in any of my hippie crap.

And when we were there, the euro was flying high. Each euro was worth two dollars—fabulous if you were European, terrible if you were American—so in addition to the inflated prices of any large city, the prices felt particularly astronomical. Unfortunately, Paris stores only hold sales twice a year. Fortunately, we were there during one of those golden moments. Unfortunately, the prices still seemed preposterous. We hobbled along the streets, our feet aching with every step, pressing our faces against the windows and sighing at the prices listed next to newer, plusher, more comfortable shoes.

Then there was the food. For a few years, my sweetie and I had followed a diet consisting mostly of meat, vegetables, and fruit. No dairy or bread.

You can guess how well this went over in Paris.

We were hungry all the time. We made it two weeks before we gave in and ate a baguette. And then another. We ate what felt like all the baguettes and cheese in Paris, and woke in the morning feeling groggy and headachy, but at least we were less hungry. Still, I lost fifteen pounds on that trip, despite my tendency to stress-eat Brie and the availability of Lemon Fanta. I should probably write an article for a women's magazine about this: "Lose Weight While Eating Your Feelings in Paris!"

I mentioned before that I didn't find Parisians as stereotypically rude. But I also found myself at odds with their mood.

I am an aggressively cheerful person (I also like mornings, so if you do not, it is probably best to avoid me until you've gotten a few cups of coffee in you). The French, especially Parisians, are. . . less so. Don't get me wrong—they are not the miserable snobs you see depicted in sitcoms. But they're not what I would call a gregariously cheerful culture.

On the train one day, a man boarded, looked at his seatmate, and blew out a contemptuous puff of air before turning away to hang up his coat. I kind of loved him for his frank, immediate dismissal of this other human being, right to his face. After all, how many times do we admonish people on the Internet, "Would you say that to someone's face?" And this guy did! You have to celebrate the unapologetic jerkishness.

We made an effort to say hello and thank you. This, of course, makes you feel fabulous and annoys the person to whom you are saying it. It's nice to say hello to a bus driver, but if the bus driver doesn't answer back, it probably has more to do with the fact that they could end up saying *bonjour* hundreds of times a day and maybe they just don't want to. When we said, *"Merci, monsieur,"* to the man running the elevator at the Eiffel Tower with one hand while scrolling through his smartphone with the other, he sighed out, *"Ouais,"* which is the French version of "yeah," the tone of which roughly translated to, "I don't even know you and I'm tired of you already." I am tempted to adopt this as my standard response to a thank-you.

And then there was the apartment.

We had rented a one-bedroom on the sixth floor of a building in Saint-Germain-des-Prés. In the pictures, it looked tiny and romantic, with a distant view of the Eiffel Tower outside the window. In reality, it was tiny and romantic. And on the sixth floor. With no elevator. We were both in reasonably good shape, but the stairs were narrow and the climb was so long and steep that when we reached the top, we had to collapse in our apartment, wheezing.

One of our neighbors had a piano. We could hear them playing some evenings as we made dinner. I have no idea how they got it up the stairs. Perhaps they brought it up key by key, and then assembled it in place.

In the corner of the bedroom was a bladeless fan. "Be careful," our landlady told us. "It's a Dyson." She said this in the same reverent tone in which one might say, "It's a Picasso." We arrived in the middle of a heat wave, which might more accurately have been referred to as a humid wave, and after walking around, we'd come back, labor up the stairs, and strip off our clothes, lying silently on the bed as the Picasso hurled the heavy air over our sticky bodies.

Paris is so far north that, in the summer, they get over sixteen hours of daylight. Miraculously, no one seems to use any of that time in the morning, but I'd look out the window to the café below at eleven P.M., when I was about to get into bed, and people would be having a leisurely dinner at the tables on the sidewalk, children playing tag among the chairs. But when I woke in the morning, feeling American and chipper and ready to Get Some Things Done, and headed out onto the streets, they were empty, and only the street sweepers and garbage men seemed to be at work. *How does anyone* function? I wondered. *Doesn't anyone have a* list?

I took six years of French in middle and high school, which qualifies me to say things such as, "How much does a stamp cost?" and "Mary listens to the radio," but renders me utterly hopeless when anyone actually responds. The best possible outcome to speaking French in Paris was that someone would hear my garbled grammar and respond in English. The wash of relief I felt whenever this happened was palpable.

In high school, I had been praised in French class for my accent. But now the elegant curls of the language sat leaden and unpronounceable on my tongue. Yet for some reason, I persisted in trying to speak French, despite the fact that everyone probably would have been happier if I had just stopped pretending I could.

But I'm betting you're noticing the pattern now. None of this was Paris's fault. I had Plans, I had Ideals, but Paris—in the way of any city, though I think this is especially true here—Paris *just doesn't care.*

Paris does not give a damn about my control issues. Paris does not give a damn about my whole-foods diet, or my minimalist shoes. Paris does not give a damn about when I think it should wake up or go to bed. Paris does not give a damn about how I think it should handle its homeless population (though, really, Paris, you need to get your act together here—it's inhumane). Paris does not give a damn about how I think it should be. Paris had been going strong for hundreds of years before I arrived and it is going to be serving crêpes and wearing insouciantly tied scarves and blowing cigarette smoke in people's faces long after I am dead.

Paris, in short, does not give a damn about me.

And you kind of have to love that.

The best trips I have taken are the ones where I have gone in with no expectations—positive or negative. Where I have read about the culture, about tipping, and adapted myself to it— flagging down waiters instead of waiting fruitlessly for them to arrive as though I were at a TGI Friday's at home, shoving into the subway along with the natives instead of waiting politely, only to be left behind on the platform, tipping the taxi driver 10 percent without feeling guilty.

This is what I should have done in Paris. I should have

adjusted to it instead of demanding it adjust to me. I should have bought new shoes. Two hundred dollars would have been a fair price for the additional walking I would have been able to do.

I should have attempted to adjust my sleep schedule to a more Parisian one. I should have recognized that the French were never going to wake up on the American side of the bed and smile at me when I wanted them to. I should have given up trying to speak French and just been grateful that so many of them speak English. I should have stopped expecting French food to fit my diet and for every morsel to be amazing and just eaten it. I should have paid less attention to my to-do list and spent more time sitting around in the Luxembourg Gardens with my face turned up to the sun.

We ended up leaving a week early (we flew directly home—I may be a fool, but I'm not an idiot). Who leaves Paris a week early? Us. We were tired, our feet hurt, I had a sore throat from all the damn bread, and I had checked off all the items on Grandma's Sightseeing Tour. When we told our landlady, she was completely stymied. "I've never heard of anyone leaving Paris early!" she said repeatedly.

Je ne sais pas, *lady*, I thought. *It's just not for me. Or maybe I'm just not for Paris.*

But the story has a happy ending. No, I didn't love the city the way my grandmother did, but when I sat down to write *The Light of Paris*, I could see every place she saw, and I could imagine her joy and excitement, and over time, I think that happiness has colored my own memories of it.

Because with some distance from the day-to-day frustrations,

I remember so much joy. When I think of Paris now, I don't think of the irritation, the confusion, the discomfort. I think of the scent of the rain-wet roses in the gardens of the Rodin museum. I think of the creaking floors in the Louvre and the little-known Picasso I fell in love with at the Centre Pompidou. I think of the best meal we had in Paris, in, of all places, a ridiculously touristy restaurant overlooking the Seine. I think of the symmetry of the endless, twisting staircase up to our apartment and the way the Eiffel Tower glowed in the not-quite-nighttime light through the window.

I think of how I was so determined to beat the crowds at Versailles that we arrived an hour before the gates opened. Not only did we beat the crowds, we were literally the first people there. We were there before the guards arrived. And we were sleep-deprived-punchy from getting up so early. My favorite picture from that trip is a selfie we took in front of the wide, deserted courtyard in front of Versailles, the palace stretching out behind us. My sweetie had said something funny—he always does—and I am laughing, my mouth wide-open, my eyes crinkled half-closed. It is my favorite picture from the trip. We look happy. We were happy. I didn't fail at Paris at all.

⚜ ⚜ ⚜

**Eleanor Brown** is the *New York Times* and international bestselling author of *The Weird Sisters* and *The Light of Paris*. She lives, writes, and teaches writing in Denver, Colorado.

*Say bonjour:*
eleanor-brown.com
Facebook: /EleanorBrownWriter
Twitter: @EleanorWrites

*The Paris Book:*
*The Light of Paris*

*I write about Paris because . . .*
More than any other city, it is a symbol of so many other things: romance, art, freedom.

*Favorite Paris moment:*
Standing in front of Van Gogh's *Starry Night Over the Rhône* in the Musée d'Orsay. It was the first time a painting had ever moved me to tears. I'll never forget it.

*Least favorite Paris moment:*
Let me just give you this piece of advice: Don't break your iPhone in France, because you'll have to deal with the Apple Store. In Paris. In French.

*Song that reminds you of Paris:*
When I took French in middle school, the audio course that went along with the textbook used snippets of "Les Champs-Élysées" as a musical interlude between exercises. I spent all six weeks of our time in Paris singing, humming, or thinking about that song. I am surprised my sweetie didn't smother me with a pillow.

*Strangest must-have travel item:*

In Europe? A washcloth. I have no idea what washcloths ever did to Europeans, but they are thin on the ground.

*In Paris, you can skip . . .*

The Louvre. I know! But it's so crowded you can't see the art, and so enormous you'll be exhausted after wandering around for hours not seeing the art. There are so many fantastic museums in the city you won't even miss it, and you can buy a Mona Lisa postcard from any street vendor and tell everyone you went.

*In Paris, you must . . .*

Sit in the shade of the trees by the Medici Fountain in the Luxembourg Gardens. Writing love poetry is optional.

⚜ ⚜ ⚜

# THE PASSION OF ROUTINE

*Jennifer L. Scott*

## Paris, 2001

When I decided to study abroad, I wanted passion, excitement, and fun. I wanted unpredictability. As a Francophile, naturally I chose Paris. In my mind, Paris was a city of romance and mystery.

But what I could never have known going into my stay was that, among many other lessons, I would learn the importance of method and order, and that true passion lies in routine. I owe this transformation to my host family, whom I'll call the Chics— Monsieur, Madame, and their son.

When I arrived in Paris, I was immediately lost on the streets of the 16th arrondissement, laden with two heavy suitcases. The taxi driver had dropped me off at what I thought was the correct building. But the street numbers in Paris don't work like they do in Southern California. So I panicked. I pictured myself sleeping in the Métro, using my two suitcases as a mattress to protect myself from the grimy floor. Then it dawned on me that I could actually call my host family with my primitive cell phone (this was 2001).

A few minutes later, Monsieur Chic found me. He was a handsome gentleman, smartly dressed in pressed trousers, a button-down shirt, a sweater, and high-quality shoes. Turns out, I was only about half a block away on the other side of the street. *Comment gênant!*—how embarrassing! I shyly greeted him, and we rode silently in the tiny elevator up to their third-floor apartment. We barely fit with my large suitcases.

When we arrived at their door, I held my breath as I walked in. This was the home I would be living in for the next six months. I had spent a lot of time picturing it in my mind: an oh-so-European minimalist flat with modern furniture. Instead, I found myself in a grand old apartment with high ceilings, walls painted a bold yellow, faded antique furniture, and aristocratic portraits adorning the hallway. It was all so much more formal than the carefree Parisian flat I had pictured in my imagination. I instantly felt self-conscious. Was I dressed properly? Had I brought the right clothes? Were these people really fancy?

Madame Chic came from the living room to greet me. I was at once struck by her style and grace. She was a quintessential Parisian lady, the kind I always envisioned: chic, elegant, and sophisticated.

Hair: short brown in a neat bob that ended just above her jawline.

Makeup: natural pink lipstick, mascara, and seemingly nothing else.

Outfit: A-line skirt, stockings, fine leather shoes, silk blouse, and pearls.

She looked crisp and confident. I was immediately intimidated.

I assumed she and Monsieur Chic must have dressed up for me, because I couldn't imagine going to such effort every day, especially just to hang out at home. But something in the back of my mind told me this was just how they were. Thankfully, I had worn a semipresentable outfit that day, but I cringed as I thought of my suitcases, which were full of ripped jeans, baggy sweats, and college tees. I couldn't imagine debuting any of those California casual looks in their grand apartment.

With a quick scan of their home, I noticed that everything was in its place. There was no clutter. Not even a little pile of papers off to the side that needed to be dealt with. It was clear that this house was run with method and order.

That first evening at dinner found me particularly nervous. My French was not very good (okay, it was practically nonexistent), and no one in *Famille* Chic spoke a word of English—not even their twenty-three-year-old son. This surprised me. Didn't everyone speak at least *some* English? And in addition to my self-consciousness regarding my conversational skills (I was certain the combination of my poor French grammar and American accent was painful for them to listen to), I was nervous because, even though this was a normal Wednesday evening, we seemed to be having a really fancy dinner party.

Monsieur Chic, the son, and I waited in the living room until dinner was announced. Madame Chic then rolled out the food on a dinner cart from the kitchen. We sat at the dining room table, which was beautifully set with cloth napkins, blue willow-patterned china, and delicately etched drinking glasses. When it was time to dish out the food, a meal in three courses, there was no free-for-all where we each grabbed a dish and plated up. As the female guest of honor, I was served first. After my turn, the food was passed around the table, ending with the son, who was at the bottom of the serving totem pole.

It was all so orderly, so *civilized*.

And *oui*, that was how we ate every single night, without exception. Madame Chic was a wonderful cook. She made the same meals in frequent rotation, but each one was a masterpiece. She prepared French classics such as coq au vin, savory tarts and crêpes, poached fish and ratatouille. (She told me she made a magnificent *boeuf bourguignon*, but I was visiting during the mad cow scare, so she refrained for the sake of the beef-phobic American.)

We began with a starter: sometimes *endive aux gratin*, sometimes a leek soup, other times a frisée salad with warm goat cheese. This was followed by the main course, one of Madame Chic's specialties. The third course was either a selection of fine cheeses that they kept at room temperature under a netted dome (Camembert being Monsieur Chic's favorite—he called it the *roi du fromage*, the "king of cheeses"), or a buttery, rich homemade tart, usually strawberry, apple, or pear.

Dinner with the Chics was my first example of the powerful combination of routine and passion. Dinner was served at the same time every evening. The food was familiar and the adherence to proper etiquette never varied, yet each of these actions produced tremendous passion around the dinner table every night. We knew what to expect, and what we were expecting was *good*.

On my first day there, Madame Chic asked me when I took my baths, in the morning or evening. I needed to choose a time to use the bathroom (there was only one bathroom for the four of us) and commit. I was initially put off by the idea of choosing my bath time. What if I changed my mind? But after living with this rigid bathroom routine, I realized the Chics scheduled their baths so they could be anticipated and enjoyed without stress or interruption.

It also turned out that I had indeed brought too many clothes with me. The wardrobe I was given to use as my closet was quite small, forcing me to live out of my suitcases for the entire semester. But as it turned out, truly, I didn't need all the clothes I had brought.

I discovered that Frenchwomen have a capsule wardrobe. They wear the same stylish, well-made clothes over and over again, but they never look shabby. *Au contraire*: They are fashionable and beautiful. After a while, I began to wonder—could I live with a ten-item wardrobe like Madame Chic and look as classy and taste-ful as she did? Sure, she had what was tantamount to a uniform— A-line skirt, silk blouse, and low heels. But she knew what she liked, what she felt good in, and stuck with it.

Living with the Chic family taught me the joy of starting my day in a refined, planned way. When I woke up every morning at around seven o'clock, Monsieur Chic and their son had al-ready left for work. Madame Chic woke up at five to make them breakfast. (*Oui*, five A.M.!)

She prepared breakfast in her quilted dressing gown to the tinkling sounds of talk radio. By the time I woke up, she was getting dressed and ready for the day. I would slip into the kitchen to eat the simple breakfast left for me: a tartine or toasted baguette with butter and homemade jam, alongside fresh fruit, petite Suisse or yogurt, and often a piece of tart from the evening before. I was served tea in a bowl. (For some reason that is still unbeknownst to me, the French take their morning tea in a bowl. But drinking it that way made me feel like a true Parisian insider!) This wasn't exactly the calorie-conscious breakfast I was used to having in California, but I wasn't about to ask Madame Chic if I could have a low-carb scramble. I figured when in Paris, I would eat breakfast as the Parisians did.

In the early evening, I helped Madame Chic prepare dinner. She enjoyed tutoring me in the art of home cooking. I noticed that she took great care in not only cooking the dish, but with its presentation. The fruit in the tart was symmetrically laid. The fruit salad (with a splash of Cointreau, her secret ingredient) was placed in an intricately etched crystal bowl. The poached fish was centered on the china platter, adorned tastefully with the delicate sauce. Every evening we feasted not only with our taste buds, but with our eyes.

While the final dinner preparations were being made, I would join Monsieur Chic and their son in the living room. Sometimes we would have an aperitif, or before-dinner drink, before being called to the table. During dinner, we engaged in passionate conversation as we enjoyed the three-course meal. After dinner, I helped

Madame Chic do the dishes, shake the tablecloth out the window, and clear the table, making everything right again. Then we joined the gentlemen in the living room while they listened to classical music on the record player, then more discussion, sometimes the evening news, and always Monsieur Chic smoking his pipe.

After a few weeks, I slowly got into the groove of living with my French family. The discomfort I had initially felt due to their foreign customs was slowly fading away. The days were organized by these seemingly contrasting concepts: routine and passion. Routine because everything was done like clockwork. There were no surprises. And passion because these routines produced the surprising effect of the deep-seated pleasure of the mundane.

Passion in the routine can be found all over Paris, not just in the Chics' apartment. Notice the patisserie workers who display their gorgeous confections in the glass, hoping to lure in customers. There is pride in their work. Regard the shopkeepers who display their beautiful fashions in the window with panache and take such pride in their own appearance. Check out the Parisians who commute to work every day and remain present while doing so, taking in the beauty of their city. While you are there, enjoy the lunch breaks, the long walks home, the beauty of the flowers displayed in the flower shops. These things will never change in Paris. There is a love of familiarity, routine, and the daily grind. There is passion, or there is nothing. We all show up every day for this life, so what is the point of merely existing? The Parisians know that to live with passion is the only way to go.

Since coming back from Paris, I have adopted Madame

Chic's Parisian routine to run my own household. Everything from breakfast to putting the last dish away at dinner is part of a delicious routine. We don't live quite as formally as the Chics did, but we do try to inject formalities into our daily routine to add a certain specialness to our day. We use Great-Grandma's delicate china and cloth napkins at dinner. We make special meals on a weeknight for no particular reason. We play classical music. I always aim to look presentable through my ten-item wardrobe and delight in everything from my nightly bath to my quick *le no makeup* routine. And while my family life can be chaotic as a working mother with a husband and three small children, I never forget the experience I had while living in Paris. I know that life at home can not only be efficient and organized, but passionate, too. And passion is what we want behind these walls, indeed.

❧ ❧ ❧

**Jennifer L. Scott** is the *New York Times* bestselling author of the Madame Chic series and creator of *The Daily Connoisseur* blog. She loves keeping in touch with readers through her weekly YouTube videos. Jennifer lives in Los Angeles with her husband and three children.

*Say bonjour:*
    jenniferlscott.com
    Facebook: /JenniferLScottAuthor
    Instagram: @DailyConnoisseur
    Twitter: @JL_Scott

*The Paris Books:*
> *Lessons from Madame Chic*
> *At Home with Madame Chic*
> *Polish Your Poise with Madame Chic*

*Favorite Paris moment:*
> One of my favorite experiences in Paris was dining at Roger la Grenouille with friends. It was the quintessential French restaurant experience. We were dressed up, the atmosphere was elegant, and the food was exquisite. It was a fabulous evening.

*Least favorite Paris moment:*
> My least favorite experience in Paris was when I was taking a bath at the Chic residence and a Parisian window washer came to the window. He must have been accustomed to happening upon unsuspecting bathers because he didn't seem fazed at all by my presence. I didn't know whether to be relieved or insulted!

*Song that reminds you of Paris:*
> Edith Piaf's *"Milord"* is just pure Paris.

*In Paris, you must . . .*
> Sit for an afternoon at a café, sipping a *café au lait*, eating a *pain au chocolat*, and people-watching (no smartphones allowed).

⚜ ⚜ ⚜

# INVESTIGATING PARIS

*Cara Black*

We never forget the feeling of a place. Paris comes to me with the scent of ripe Montreuil peaches, the high heels clicking over the cobbles, the dripping plane tree branches leaving shadows on the *quai*, the flowing, khaki-colored Seine. Always the shiver from cold stone inside soot-stained, centuries-old churches, relics of history and mystery under a piercing blue sky. But feeling Paris is not the same as knowing it, and I have spent my life trying to connect to this city as one of my own.

I first came to Paris in a long-ago September. What I owned lay in my rucksack carried on my back. My travel mate and I woke up in the École de Médecine's student dormitory somewhere in the Latin Quarter. Two medical students, who were on call all night, had given us their beds. Needless to say, they expected to share them with us the following morning. I remember that peculiar feeling of a fluffy duvet, sun pouring in the tall window, and two grinning male students greeting us with soup bowls of bitter coffee, and peaches. Peaches whose sweet juice stained our chins. We thanked them, maneuvering our way out by promising to come back. Somehow we never did.

That first September, wearing a déclassé flannel shirt and jeans, I'd sought out the famous Prix Goncourt award-winning writer Romain Gary. His book *Promise at Dawn*, read when I was a teenager, opened the door to writing for me. His prose and the story inspired me.

He'd answered my fan letter with a handwritten note, including his return address on the envelope. Needless to say, I took that as an invitation—one does that when one is young—and knocked on his enormous carved wooden door, inside a seventeenth-century limestone building on the Left Bank, carrying a bunch of orange marigolds from the market.

"Do I know you?" asked the man who answered—a black-haired man with a matching mustache and amazing aquamarine eyes full of curiosity.

Stumbling and tongue-tied, I realized I had made a terrible faux pas—he received fan mail from all over the world. My brash confidence, whether from youth, naiveté, or both, came crashing around me. Who was I to assume I could deal with those medical students and a famous author like this?

"Just a moment," he said, and shut the door. Mortified, I turned down the creaking wood hallway in the glow of an Art Nouveau stained-glass window, trying to make myself small and escape down the spiral staircase. But he emerged a moment later. "Would you like a coffee?"

I nodded and managed, "Sure." Minutes later we were off,

down the narrow rue du Bac and into the corner café, his local, where a cigar and espresso awaited him on the zinc counter.

"And for her?" the man behind the counter asked Monsieur Gary.

"She'll have the same."

So I smoked my first cigar and drank my first espresso with a famous French writer, standing at the counter, trying not to choke or wince at the tiny, bitter cup of coffee, and desperately struggling to sound intelligent.

But he made no mention of my clumsy attempts at sophistication. A truly generous man, he told me about his life; how he'd just separated from his wife, the actress Jean Seberg; and the heating problems he had with his house in Majorca. A mix of the "normal" for the famous writer.

We didn't talk about writing, though I wish we had. Yet that meeting in the café encouraged my resolve that I would write someday. But it wasn't until years later in Paris, during another September, that I found a story. My friend Sarah took me to the Marais, then ungentrified, and showed me where her mother, at the age of fourteen, had hidden during the German occupation. Sarah's mother's family had been taken by the French police and she'd lived, hidden, wearing a yellow star and going to school, until the Liberation of Paris. Sadly, her family never returned.

The war had never felt close to me until that moment, standing on the narrow rue des Rosiers in front of a building where a tragedy—probably so many more than one in this old Jewish part of Paris—had occurred. It was the collision between the present and the past that floated in front of me as I imagined

Sarah's mother's life. Almost as if the ghosts hovered out of reach, but there in the shadowy stone recesses of the building. I never forgot that shiver of encountering the past.

A fascination with Paris is a family trait. My uncle and my father, two brothers from Chicago with not a French vein in their bodies, were devoted Francophiles. As a child my father had read me Charles Dickens's *A Tale of Two Cities*, a nineteenth-century edition illustrated with scary woodcuts. In that story, Paris was peopled by revolutionaries, men in frock coats, and Madame Defarge knitting with a malevolent eye.

My uncle, who lived with us, had stayed on the Left Bank. "Studying art," he claimed, but really drinking a lot of *vin rouge*. He'd talk about how, after a night of partying, they'd end up at five A.M. in their tuxedoes at Les Halles, Paris's famous fresh food market, where they'd eat onion soup next to the butchers working in their bloodstained aprons. How his teacher Georges Braque's studio was so cold, and the artist such a tightwad, that when my uncle asked the master to put more coals in the stove because the model was turning blue, Braque gestured for him to leave and kicked him downstairs. His stories offered an earthy side to the photos I'd seen in *Vogue*, with slim, tousle-haired women, effortlessly chic in Chanel jackets, carrying dogs in their handbags. The glamor and the grit seemed to go hand in hand.

When my father heard the story of Sarah's mother hiding in the Marais during the war, he handed me a slim crime novel by Georges Simenon and said, "Read this. It's set in Paris."

*But it's old-fashioned*, I thought.

"It might be a way to tell this story you're going on about," said my father, so tired of the obsession consuming me after hearing about Sarah's family.

So I blame my entry into crime writing on Inspector Maigret, the protagonist for Georges Simenon's novels about a Parisian police inspector. Georges Simenon, originally from Belgium, first arrived in Paris as an outsider. While Agatha Christie is known all over the world as the queen of crime, George Simenon has sold almost as many books—between 500 and 700 million copies worldwide of his 570 books.

His Inspector Maigret novels captured my imagination. Could I approach understanding Parisians like an investigation, a case to crack like those slender Inspector Maigret novels that intrigued me? Maybe I could understand Parisians, blend in at least for a moment before I opened my mouth. Figure out the code they communicated in, discover if their flair disguised another reality. The seething passions below the surface that led to spilling blood. What better way than an investigation for someone like me—not as a voyeur but as an observer who noted details, caught a nuance, dug below the surface, always searching for motive, opportunity?

I identified with an investigator because I was always on the outside looking for a way in. And crime fiction sets Paris against a backdrop of gray, an overcast sky, and perhaps a corpse or two in the cobbled streets—discovered, of course, by Georges Simenon's pipe-smoking Inspector Jules Maigret.

Though Maigret's era passed long ago, it's not all history. His "old office" in the police department at 36 Quai des Orfévres, the Paris Préfecture (often referred to as "36"), now belongs to a trim fortysomething *commissaire* with a laptop; gone is the charcoal-burning stove. Maigret's unit, the Sûreté, is no more, but has been restructured and renamed the Brigade Criminelle, Paris's elite homicide squad. From time immemorial, officers have hung bloody clothing from crime scenes to dry under the rafters in the attic at 36. This tradition hasn't changed. Nor has the rooftop view, courteously shown to me by a member of the Brigade Criminelle. A vista with the Seine and all of Paris before us. Breathtaking. And beneath us are 36's underground holding cells, which date from the Revolution, if not further back.

That's become my job: to write stories about crime and murder *à la parisienne*, set in contemporary Paris. A way for me, an outsider, to explore and scratch that itch of curiosity.

The streets are the same as they were in Maigret's time, but today's Fifth Republic Paris is a blended wealth of cultural traditions from all over the world. For me, this means there are new enclaves and hidden worlds to encounter no matter how well I think I know these cobbled streets.

To know Paris, as Edmund White and countless others have observed, one must be a *flâneur*, taking leisurely strolls through the city, letting the unexpected moods wash over you and remaining open to discovery—in my case, with an eye for crime. One must take the pulse of a *quartier*, assessing its rhythm; know it by heart, from the lime trees flanking its boulevards to its nineteenth-century *passages couverts*. Only when I can feel that pulse can I start the rest of my research for a novel.

Writers, like detectives, must be curious, ask, "What if?," which I had been doing since I first stepped on the cobbles.

Detectives follow their noses, as the old adage goes; when a word rings false, when the indefinable something-isn't-right moment happens—that is the moment to wonder, to ask questions. The exchange of a furtive glance, a figure ducking out of sight into the back of a café and failing to reemerge. In Paris, those who want to disappear can do so via the spare exit gate of a back courtyard, the city's series of covered passageways, even over the gray zinc rooftops or underground through a cellar or an old World War II bomb shelter.

All a writer needs is that "what if," and a story tumbles out. I imagine the line at the *tabac* by Pigalle Métro station evaporating, the group of teens breaking off into threes to pickpocket unsuspecting tourists; an artist in a tiny fifth-floor den closing her shutters to block out street noise; a man entering a jewelry store in the "golden triangle" off the Champs-Élysées with a gun to perform one in a series of daytime robberies. How I long to get it right, to write about the city with the confidence of a native to reflect the Paris of the 1990s with its hidden courtyards and criminal underbelly—updating the Paris Inspector Maigret had haunted.

Over the years I'd gotten to meet police, and in order to know more I'd gone out drinking with the *flics*, the local cops. Lucky enough to receive such an invitation one night, I joined several at the bar across the Seine from 36, where they'd taken over a back table.

An intoxicated young man looking for a fight entered the bar and approached us at our table—a table of off-duty police officers. Who knows why? Bad luck, I suppose. He began a drunken monologue. If you've had such an encounter, you know the kind.

This young man was the sort you wanted to leave before he got belligerent. A few of the officers spoke with him and escorted him out. He sat down on the sidewalk outside, and one of the admin police, who resembled an accountant, stayed behind to join him on the curb across from *la maison*, as the Préfecture is called. This policeman spoke with him for a long time amid the smokers and passersby, talking him down rather than talking down to him. I'd gone outside for a cigarette and noticed them carrying on a conversation. I didn't get involved, as I didn't have anything to add, nor did I wish to accidentally provoke someone so inebriated. When I came out again later, they were still talking. The *flic* was kindly asking questions now. Maybe the kid had broken up with his girlfriend, lost his job, or just had a really bad day; I never found out.

It was something the *flic* didn't have to do, with all his buddies inside drinking. Whether he enjoyed getting out of the bar, or the view of the Seine, or just talking with this kid, it really struck me as something Jules Maigret would have done. Maigret, the knowing, sometimes fatherly figure who knew people would tell you their story if you just coaxed it out of them. Averting disaster, heading off a confrontation, recognizing the signs that a situation could spin out of control. Maybe that was part of what they taught at the police academy. By the time the young man (who was still, in my opinion, one slice short of a baguette, sobriety-wise) finally left, he had a smile on his face. I'll never know what happened to him after that, but I had the feeling he would just go home and sleep it off. He wouldn't feel denigrated or demoralized in the morning, except for a hangover.

Georges Simenon's novels are full of investigators, *flics* on their daily beat, the victims' neighbors, hotel concierges, capturing a time, a part of Paris that exists now only in the imagination. A time when cell phones and numeric entry keypads were unheard-of—one could only ring the concierge's bell to gain entry after midnight. Everyone knew everyone else's business in a city with enclosed courtyards, high walls, and watchful eyes. I think they still do. Parisians smoked and drank morning, noon, and night. Men's wool overcoats and hats steamed as they came in from a wet winter evening to a warm café with a charcoal stove burning. People knew their neighbors. Snitches snitched. Girlfriends chatted with one another and mothers-in-law complained—human connections abounded, often forming a web of lies and deceit.

In that complicated world, Maigret keeps at it—plodding, questioning, then throwing out those questions, lighting his pipe when it goes out, and the suspect in the chair opposite him knows it's only a matter of time. As does Maigret. He drinks at lunch, sometimes he gets angry, even orders sandwiches and beer in the afternoon. He takes the annual August *vacances* with Madame Maigret unless a case comes up—but when doesn't it?—and detains him in hot, deserted Paris. But a few of his investigations find him out in the countryside, in hermetically sealed villages where observant eyes don't miss a thing. As in many cultures, an outsider arriving in a small French village is often met with distrust, even more so if they're different.

That hasn't changed.

I confess that when I first began writing my Aimée Leduc novels, I would think, *Okay. There's a murder, a staircase dripping with blood . . . what would Inspector Maigret do?* That wasn't always much help, since Aimée is a PI, not a policewoman. But then I'd consider what she might do if Maigret appeared on the scene and questioned her after she found the body. That worked a little better. Of course, the police system in place now is different: Jules Maigret, as the head *commissaire*, would certainly not respond in person. Today, it would be the Brigade Criminelle and *le procureur* (the equivalent of our DA) who would hotfoot it to the scene and dictate the next steps in the investigation. I had to change my way of thinking about police process in a murder investigation, my *flic* friends told me. The way Maigret operated didn't make for a plausible scenario now. So I relearned in order to keep the details in my books accurate, and came to the conclusion that Maigret had it easier than a head *commissaire* would today.

Is Simenon's work dated? Historical? Timeless? I'd argue the second two. I personally like my Paris streets dark and narrow, with glistening cobbles. The air thick with mist and suspicion. The Montmartre cemetery wall, the same as it was then, hulking with old, lichen-covered stone. I've imagined a corpse there more than once. My friend lives a block away, and returning late at night from the last Métro, walking uphill from Place de Clichy, the cinéma marquees dark, the café lights fading as I cross over the cemetery, I hear the thrum of the old Citroën or Renault engine, the shift of gears, and smell the cherry tobacco (I like to think Maigret smoked cherry tobacco, though I don't know that it's ever specified; perhaps there's a Simenon scholar out there who can tell me). Flashlights illuminate the corpse sprawled on the damp pavement; Maigret nods to his lieutenant with a "Take this down," and we're off on an investigation. An investigation that leads to the hidden life behind the walls, intrigue in the *quartier*, and worlds we'd never visit otherwise. Worlds that make me feel like I belong.

The iconic Préfecture at 36 Quai des Orfèvres is now falling to pieces, the *flics* say—well-worn and tired around the edges, ancient and unequipped to handle the new technology the force needs. They're moving to a brand-new building that's designed to gather all the gendarme divisions in one place. It's in the 17th near the Batignolles park, and the old train switching yards, abandoned for many years. Had France gotten the 2012 Olympic bid that went to England, this was where the Olympic Village would have been. I'm kind of glad that never happened. As some *flics* point out, the move has been long slated, but with the current budget crisis, there's an advantage to keeping the current headquarters. The genius of being in the very center of Paris is that the city Tribunal is right next door. Prisoners awaiting trial literally go from their holding cells to the court through an ancient underground tunnel. A friend, a *flic* whose first assignment out of the academy was escorting those in custody from their ancient, funky cells to the court, aptly described the surroundings as "medieval," as ancient and foreboding as they were in Maigret's time.

On boulevard Richard Lenoir is where the inspector lived with Madame Maigret. I confess to making a pilgrimage to their apartment building. While I know it's a fictional building, I couldn't resist scoping it out. I imagined myself saying, "It would be this street number and, yes, just as Simenon described." Years later, riding a Vélib, a cycle from the citywide bike share, I returned home late to find that all the stations near my lodgings on the Canal Saint-Martin were full. *Zut!* It was late and drizzling, and I was hungry and looking to rest my aching feet. Finally, I found a single empty spot for my bicycle: on boulevard Richard Lenoir, right below the Maigret apartment. How I wished Madame Maigret were still up waiting for Jules, warming a pot of cassoulet on the stove.

Even though I've made regular visits to France for over twenty years, I'm still *l'américaine.* I've been a guest at several of the locals' weddings, heard about their husbands' affairs . . . I'd like to think they trust me now. After all, I've been into their homes, which is considered an honor and no mean feat. But in many ways I'm still the outsider, the investigator. And yet they've given me a window into their lives, a way to see, so if that's the way an outsider is, then I'm fine with it. I think if I ever do completely understand the French, the magic will be gone—but no fear of that. The first peaches of the season still drip and stain my chin, I'm full of wonder, and that duvet feels comfortable now.

⚜ ⚜ ⚜

**Cara Black** is the *New York Times* bestselling author of the Aimée Leduc series, and was awarded the Medaille de la Ville de Paris for contributions to French culture. She's a dog owner with nomadic tendencies and drinks too much espresso.

**Say bonjour:**

carablack.com
Facebook: /CaraBlackAuthor
Instagram: @carablack51
Twitter: @carablack

**The Paris Books:**

17 books in the Aimée Leduc investigations series set
in Paris, including:
*Murder in Saint Germain*
*Murder in the Marais*
*Murder on the Quai*

**Favorite Paris moment:**

Favorite walk? If it was good enough for Victor
Hugo, it's good enough for me: visiting Place des
Vosges. The seventeenth-century square feels like it
was built for *flâneurs*, and I never feel more
European than I do in this square and the adjoining
garden of Hôtel de Sully next door and its wonderful
hidden bookshop.

**Least favorite Paris moment:**

Being late to the January and July sales—*soldes*—
everything has been picked over and is still too
expensive anyway.

**Favorite book about Paris:**

Mavis Gallant's story "The Other Paris," in the 1953
*New Yorker*. She's an amazing writer, and to me,

touches the soul of the City of Light and the love affair expats have with it.

*Song that reminds you of Paris:*

"Menilmontant," written by Charles Trenet and sung by Yves Montand. This ballad takes me there, to the hilly, still cobbled streets of Menilmontant.

*Favorite non-Paris travel destination:*

Favignana island off the coast of Sicily.

*In Paris, don't bother . . .*

The Ferris wheel in Place de la Concorde isn't recommended for queasy stomachs. Try hiking up the Arc de Triomphe for a better view of Paris.

*In Paris, you must . . .*

Shop at the Marche d'Aligre in the 12th arrondissement. It's the oldest market in Paris and where real Parisians shop. Then go around the corner to le Baron Rouge, a great wine bar, and try the oysters.

⚜ ⚜ ⚜

# MY PARIS DREAMS

## M.J. Rose

I never believed in magic, but my great-grandmother did. Annie Berger was a self-proclaimed witch and uncanny fortune-teller, and it is her history that has inspired so many of my novels—as has Paris, where she was born and lived as a young girl.

I grew up hearing stories about Grandma Berger's City of Light, stories she always told me with a gleam in her eye.

"Dreams will come true for you in Paris," she said once, when she was using tarot cards to tell my fortune.

But they never did.

I was fourteen the first time I visited Paris, staying with my parents at the Ritz hotel in Place Vendôme. In the bathroom, water poured from the mouths of gold swan faucets. On the bed was a duvet filled with down feathers, softer and far more luxurious than my wool blanket at home.

Our suite was on the second floor—an easy walk to the lobby—except why walk when you could glide up and down in an old-fashioned gilded cage, an elevator complete with a white-gloved attendant? And especially when that attendant was young and, to me, exceptionally attractive. I'd always loved watching old black-and-white movies and he looked like a cross between a young Gregory Peck and Montgomery Clift.

I can picture him still, all these years later. He was tall and gangly, with fair skin and black hair. And he had a mole high on his left cheekbone. He wore a formal navy uniform with brass buttons, complete with epaulets and a round cap with the name of the hotel elegantly embroidered on the front.

When we stepped into the elevator, and during the ride down, he always stared straight ahead. Never spoke. Never made eye contact with any of us. Just lifted his gloved hand and pressed the appropriate button on the highly polished brass panel—which mirrored his image, as I discovered on my second trip up with him.

I noticed the panel. Realized I could see his reflection. And then became aware that he was looking at me. Instantly and completely, I fell in love. Why we fall in love is often a mystery. Certainly why a teenage girl from Manhattan would fall in love with a Parisian elevator boy remains one to this day.

So that I could see him more often, every evening I wrote five or six postcards, and all the next day brought them downstairs to mail. One at a time. Over the course of a day, I managed to take the elevator up and down at least a dozen times.

I wanted him to say hello. And then maybe stop the elevator and kiss me. I'd never been kissed—but there were all those black-and-white movies running through my mind.

Ours was not an unrequited love. He never took his eyes off me in that golden mirror. But I supposed he wanted to keep his job, so he never made the first move.

Finally, on the last day, I decided to say something. But what? I practiced a half dozen sentences in my mediocre French. I wrote out my address on one of the postcards. I put it in my pocketbook, prepared to give it to him on my final trip down to the lobby. At least I could do that.

But when the time came, I couldn't do it. Or I didn't do it. I was too shy.

It was my first experience with a certain kind of thwarted romance, but not my last. My first and not last experience with certain men who, no matter where I met them, I always called my "Paris boyfriends." They were men I was attracted to and who clearly were attracted to me, but for whatever reason waited for me to make the first move. Which I couldn't do.

I've always been outspoken. Bold and brazen and aggressive in so many ways. When I was only twenty-five, I became one of the youngest creative directors in advertising history. Years later, in the 1990s, I became the first novelist to use the Internet to publish an eBook, which was picked up by a New York publisher. I take pride in breaking rules. Politically, socially, and with fashion, I've always marched to my own drummer.

But I have also always been bizarrely shy when it comes to making the first move with a man. Not the second . . . or the third . . . but that first one . . . just can't do it.

Over the years, Paris became the city of my soul. Each time I visited, my first morning there I'd walk out into the middle of the Pont Royal, look out at the skyline to the left and then the right, breathe in the perfumed air, and weep. Cry with joy just to be there.

My great-grandmother said my dreams would come true in her City of Light. But her prediction still had not come to pass when I visited Paris on a business trip shortly before I left advertising.

That April, I was there to shoot a perfume commercial with a French production company for a multi-international fragrance company. Along with four colleagues, I was staying for two weeks—five days of prepping, three of shooting. With a weekend in the middle. I was happy to be in my favorite city. Happy to be taking a break from a job that I'd been doing for a long time and that wasn't a challenge anymore, from my lackluster marriage and my therapist and my efforts to come to terms with the fact that I was in a troubled relationship that kept me from dreaming.

Our team stayed at the Lenox, a small Left Bank boutique hotel with charming rooms and a terrific art deco bar downstairs that doubled as a breakfast room.

Every night after work, before dinner, we'd gather for drinks, usually joined by our client, the film company's producer, and the director, Jacques R. He was an accomplished and iconoclastic filmmaker who had directed several award-winning film noir movies but only a few select commercials. The provocative concept my co–creative director and I had come up with for this new perfume was perfect for his style.

Jacques spoke excellent English, albeit with a heavy French accent. And he looked every bit the part of a filmmaker. Wiry, with dirty blond hair and dark blue eyes, he always wore a uniform of black leather motorcycle jacket, black scarf, white T-shirt, and black jeans. Whenever he joined us for cocktails, he always ordered Champagne—my preferred drink as well.

Our prep went well, and we had the weekend off before start-ing shooting on Monday. During the break, my art director, pro-ducer, and account executive were going off to do tourist things. That left me blissfully free to be by myself in my favorite city, to just wander and wonder.

Saturday morning, I went to the Musée de l'Orangerie to commune with Monet's water lilies, a kind of shrine for me. The murals reach into my soul and twist my heart. That the artist could create such overwhelming beauty while going blind moved me profoundly. The determination and willpower Monet drew on to create these masterpieces usually inspired me, but that morning it admonished me, reminding me I'd given up any effort to fulfill my own artistic dreams . . . dropped them at the door of the ad agency, which required a sixty-, sometimes seventy-hour workweek.

Leaving the museum, I walked through the Tuileries, to-ward the Louvre, planning to have a late breakfast at Café Marly. It wasn't crowded yet, and I had no trouble obtaining a table by the windows. I ordered coffee and an omelet. Just after the food arrived, the waiter brought over a glass of Champagne. When I told him I hadn't ordered it, he smiled, and nodded behind him and to the left.

"From Monsieur," he said.

I looked over and saw Jacques, camera around his neck over his scarf, tipping his own glass to me. He rose and came over to say hello. I asked him to join me and we fell into an easy conver-sation about work, which led him to ask where the rest of my team was. I explained about the tourist excursions and how since

I'd been to Paris so many times before, I had chosen to spend the day on my own.

"My son's mother has him for the weekend and I've been out shooting," Jacques said.

"Even on your day off?"

"I'm always happiest behind a lens. If you're free after your meal, since you've seen tourist Paris, would you like to see some of my secret city?"

His words thrilled me almost like an embrace. Was there a seductive tone to the invitation or was it just my imagination?

Jacques said he'd parked his Vespa on the other bank in front of a friend's shop, so after he paid my bill, as well as his own, we headed for the Pont des Arts. Paris is a city of lovers. But as we walked across the bridge, I noticed what seemed like even more couples than usual holding hands or stopping to kiss.

I assumed Jacques was so used to them he wasn't even aware of them. Was I more conscious of them because my own life was so unromantic? I'd had a decent marriage, but never a passionate one. My then husband and I were both workaholics who'd focused more on our careers than our relationship. But in the last year I'd realized our time apart was camouflaging a more serious problem. At our cores, we were badly mismatched. I always saw the proverbial glass-half-full but he was an inveterate pessimist and it made me profoundly sad.

Suddenly, I wanted what these lovers had. Someone to capture me in an embrace on a bridge while dozens of people passed by, because nothing else mattered but our lips finding each other's.

On the other side of the Pont, Jacques unlocked his shiny black Vespa, parked in front of a small apartment building, put on a matching helmet, and gave me one, too. "Hop on and hold on," Jacques instructed.

I did as he said, throwing my leg over the seat, finding footholds, and then putting my arms around him, all too aware of my torso pressed up against his back. Even with his heavy leather jacket and my rain coat between us, I felt naked.

We took off, zipping in and out of traffic, whizzing through sections of the city that passed by so fast I hardly had time to register where we were. I hadn't been on a bike since college, and it was exhilarating. The thrum of the engine sending vibrations up my legs, the powerful thrust of the machine, all much more erotic than I remembered. Or maybe it was the company?

Finally we stopped. I didn't recognize the area. He parked and led me down an alley. The street sign read "passage du Désir." Halfway down the block, he stopped at a chocolatier. The scent enveloped me even before we stepped inside. The smell was intoxicating and mysterious. From the look of the display cases, the tile floor, and the mercury-mirrored walls, the shop seemed to have been there for at least a hundred years.

"If it's all right, I'm going to buy my favorites for you. Yes?"

I nodded.

Jacques and the proprietor spoke too quickly for me to pick up much of what was said. I watched her put six oblong pieces of shiny dark chocolate into a silver sack and affix a purple label on it to keep it closed. Then she put six round balls of a dusty, darker chocolate into a second bag, securing it the same way.

Outside on the street, Jacques opened one of the sacks and pulled out a piece of chocolate.

"Open your mouth and close your eyes. Don't bite on it at first, just let it melt. There's an art to eating fine chocolate."

I did as I was told and he fed me. The taste was very intense. Bitter, melting silk, and then the surprise hint of citrus. My body reacted to the delectable flavor and to the intimacy of the act. I was surprised at the power of my reaction and scared as I realized how happy it was making me. The emotions were unexpected and complicated and, for so many reasons, wrong. But I knew every part of me hungered for more of it.

"Once the chocolate covering melts . . . chew," he instructed.

I shivered at his words as I did as he said and bit down on the soft, sour candied peel. I experienced the taste with a jolt of pleasure far more intense than I'd expected.

When I finished, he steered me out of the passage at the other end, then down one street and then another until we reached our next destination. The short street looked fairly ordinary. Apartment houses lined both sides. A gothic church sat at its end.

"What's here?"

Jacques pointed to the street sign—rue de la Fidélité.

"Oh, and we were just in passage du Desir," I said.

"You catch on quick." He smiled.

So did I. "And where are we going next?" I asked.

"You'll see."

We were heading toward a church. Jacques told me that in its first iteration, in the sixth century, it had been a monastery, then was rebuilt in 1180 and yet again in the fifteenth century.

He peppered his history lesson with the story of a parishioner, a young widow, who, in 1633, with the help of her confessor Vincent de Paul, created the order of Daughters of Charity to help the poor and care for the sick. The community, he told me, had spread to all corners of the world and was still active in areas as far away as Israel, the Americas, and Australia.

"They say her body," Jacques whispered in a forced dramatic sotto voce, "is incorruptible. She's been nominated for sainthood."

We'd reached the end of the street, where he pointed to the sign.

"Here we are. From desire to fidelity and now we're on rue de Paradis."

Not the way I'd experienced my romantic life, I thought. Desire for my husband had led to fidelity but not to paradise. I smiled while at the same time feeling tears well up. Blinking them away, I looked at the window display Jacques was pointing out.

Every store on the street was dedicated to the *arts de table*. Each window displayed crystal or china. The buildings were a combination of styles from the last hundred years; the passage of time visible in the tile work, stained glass, and other architectural details.

Jacques led me into the Baccarat store. As we walked through the elegant lobby, its giant glittering chandelier cast tiny rainbows on the floor and walls, even on our faces and hands.

"Come, they have a museum. I want to show you something."

Inside a large high-ceilinged room, there were cases and cases of historical objects, all produced by the glass manufacturer, dating back to the late 1700s. Weaving through them, he led me deeper into the museum.

He knew just where he was going. Finally, we stopped. My eyes were already glazed over from all the dazzling crystal.

"These glasses," he said, pointing at a set of goblets, "were made by Count Thierry for his mistress in 1826."

I looked at the wine and water goblets. Five sizes, each a watery shade of pale blue, highly faceted with ornate silver filigree work on the stem.

"The count had the glass matched to his lover's eyes and ordered more than one thousand of them in the years they were together. Only these six still exist. All the others were smashed."

"Why?"

"The count was so jealous he didn't want anyone to drink from a glass touched by his lover's lips. Each goblet she drank from was destroyed after she used it. Love," Jacques said, "to the point of madness—or else what is the point of love?" And then he smiled.

Was that how he loved? I wondered. I wanted to know so badly. What if I just asked him? And yet I couldn't, I didn't dare. I didn't know how to take that step into unknown territory.

Back on the bike we rode to 3 avenue Franklin D. Roosevelt and then walked toward the Palais de la Découverte. We stopped at a small white statue of the Swiss Alps in front of vine-covered columns and a stone staircase seemingly leading nowhere. After descending the broken steps, we walked through an archway into another world. A wilderness. The sounds of traffic from the Champs-Élysées were gone, magically replaced by bird calls and splashing water.

Maples, lilacs, bamboo, vines heavy with wisteria, perfumed the air with a heady sweet, peppery scent. We were lost in green. Awash in nature. There in the middle of Paris we'd found an overgrown garden, magnificent in its obsolescence.

Past a wooden footbridge, we wandered through arches overgrown with ivy. A meandering pathway led to a pond, where we stopped to watch the last rays of sun illuminate the orange carp as they slowly circled their home.

I was so aware of Jacques beside me and so curious about what was on his mind. What did he want? What did this day mean to him? Probably nothing but a little distraction, I thought. The paucity of romance in my life was making me overly sensitive and overly reactive.

We continued on. The quiet was profound now. Rock alcoves offered benches, but we kept walking past the pond until we reached an Art Nouveau sculpture full of beautiful women in bas relief against a large swirling sweep of white marble.

"It's entitled *The Poet's Dream*. An homage to Alfred de Musset. Quite a romantic one, too—look at him daydreaming about all these lovely women. It's said that each was one of the loves of his life."

Orange and lemon trees scented the air. A bird whistled. The stream rushed by. We wandered on the twisting path.

Back on the bike, Jacques drove across the bridge and headed toward Notre-Dame, stopping three times at various shops. When we arrived at our destination, the square du Vert-Galant at the tip of the Île de la Cité, we had a feast: a bottle of Champagne, peaches, cheese, and a fresh baguette.

He uncorked the bottle and handed it to me.

"This spot was made famous by King Henri IV. A most amorous ruler. They called him Le Vert Galant—the grand spark. He was notorious for his sexual exploits. His appetite was insatiable. He kept several mistresses at a time and still visited brothels."

"And this place?"

"He loved the view and thought it very romantic. But as for what went on here? You'd have to get the trees to tell you."

We ate the crusty bread, soft cheese, and ripe fruit and drank the Champagne. As we sat and looked out at the Seine, clouds rolled across the sky and a storm blew in. When the rain came, we huddled beneath a broad chestnut tree, the water releasing the leaves' sweet smell. We watched the swans swim by, as untroubled by the rain as we were.

"They mate for life," Jacques said.

For a moment, I thought he was going to kiss me, and I wondered if I'd taste the wine on his lips. But there was no kiss.

*Just do it—reach out and touch him*, I commanded myself. And then almost laughed out loud realizing each of those phrases had come from a different commercial. The first Nike, the second AT&T. I was a casualty of advertising. Jacques quoted poetry. My mind went to Madison Avenue slogans. But that thought was just a distraction from how disappointed I was, once again, in myself and my timidity.

"Have you ever been here, on the Île?" he asked when the rain stopped.

"No."

"I live here and it's like a little secret in the middle of a city that is full of secrets. Come, there's one more secret I want to show you."

He led me down two picturesque streets lined with three- and four-story buildings, with overflowing window boxes and elaborate wrought-iron doors. We passed art galleries, ice cream shops, and an antique poster and photography gallery, where we spent a half hour in the fourteenth-century building looking at old photos of Picasso, Matisse, and Monet, and posters by Pal and Mucha.

We wound up at Mélodies Graphiques, a store that sold beautiful stationery and journals, special pens, and inks in jewel tones—from ruby to turquoise to emerald.

Jacques took my arm. "Come, you have to see the pièce de résistance."

On a table in the back of the store, an oversize book—at least three hundred pages—sat open. A chartreuse ribbon ran down the middle of the page. There were entries in various colored inks, all in different handwriting.

"It's a lovers' assignation book. For over a hundred years, people have come here and left messages for each other."

*Meet me later at our place.*

*I'll be at the restaurant tomorrow.*

*I'm at home tonight alone.*

I ran my finger down the satin ribbon. The words blurring. I wasn't sure why the tears came. Was it because suddenly I was so viscerally aware of what I was missing, or because I found the story so touching? Jacques noticed and smiled in a way that told me he understood exactly and precisely, and then he pulled out a handkerchief and handed it to me.

"For your tears," he said softly.

There was another moment when I thought he was going to lean down and kiss me. But he didn't. Maybe he was waiting for me to make that first move. After all, I was the one who was married. And I was the creative director of the ad agency that had hired him.

I desperately wanted to lean in. The seconds passed. Neither of us said a word. The world continued to rotate but I stayed frozen in place.

And then the storekeeper called out, "Can I help you?"

Jacques said something to him in French and we left the store. I was in the kind of stupor that a sudden rush of excitement leaves you with.

Outside, dusk was falling. *L'heure bleue*—the blue hour, they call it in Paris. A time so lovely, Guerlain had named one of its perfumes after it.

"Do you have plans?" Jacques asked.

I nodded. "At eight. A dinner with the client." As I said it, I wished I hadn't. Wished I had said, *No, I have nothing to do but spend more time with you.*

"Time then for one last glass of Champagne." Jacques took my arm. Even through his jacket and my coat, the connection burned. Was I the only one to feel it?

"I know just the place," he said.

It looked like a houseboat. One of hundreds dotting the Seine. But it was a bar. There were only locals there, and they knew Jacques and brought the Champagne without him ordering it.

While the night sky turned dark, we talked about art, photography, perfume, and advertising. He told me his stories and I told him mine the way you do when you're with someone new. Everything is fascinating and interesting and curious.

And then the day was over.

❦

I never made that first move. It would have been so nice to have a romantic adventure in the city of romance. To have a dream come true. But it wasn't meant to be. I had another Paris boyfriend to add to my list of missed opportunities.

I didn't get back to Paris for two years, and then was invited to attend a birthday bash for a dear friend who lived in Fontainebleau—just a half hour outside of Paris. I'd been divorced for six months and it seemed like the perfect excursion.

I planned to spend two days before the party and three days after by myself in the city. Once again, I was staying at the Lenox on rue de l'Université. Once again, I was aware of every couple I saw kissing and holding hands, each one reminding me of my recent failed marriage.

For the first time, Paris seemed melancholy. It rained every day and was cold. The birthday bash had been spoiled by my friend's father-in-law being rushed to the hospital after what turned out to be a heart attack.

Back in the city, I spent Monday afternoon wandering. I wound up on the Île Saint-Louis and passed the stationery store that Jacques R. had showed me. I went inside. I examined all the beautiful papers and bottles of fancifully colored ink, thinking that shops like this only existed in European cities anymore. A store dedicated to handwriting with fountain pens on exquisite paper and fine leather journals. I looked at packets of pencils and rubber stamps and elaborate ribbons.

I walked to the back of the store. The reason I'd gone inside in the first place. To see if the Lovers' Journal, as I'd come to think of it, was still there. And it was. And it was open to a page empty except for that day's date on the top. I hesitated. Then picked up a pen, dipped it into a bottle of deep red ink, and wrote.

*Love to the point of madness—or else what is the point of love? Jacques, I'm in Paris. At the Lenox. I'll be at the bar at 6 PM.*

It was a silly and overly romantic and impossible gesture. Of course he would never read it. If I really wanted to see him, I could have called him on the phone. But that was taking that first step I'd never known how to take. This was leaving it not just to fate but to magic. To my great-grandmother's magic. Which I wanted to believe in—but didn't really. Couldn't really. There'd never been any proof.

That night, even though I knew better, I went to the bar at six P.M., sat at a table for two, ordered my glass of Champagne, and waited. Of course Jacques didn't come. I had been foolish to think he would. As foolish as I'd been to think that elevator boy was going to turn around and kiss me.

The next day I went to the d'Orsay and afterward walked in the rain through the Tuileries. I wandered around the Left Bank, bought a scarf in one shop, an antique pin in another. I didn't have any plans for that night, so I bought some cheese at Androuet, the hundred-year-old shop off rue du Bac, and a baguette at the bakery on the corner, and headed back to the hotel.

On the way to the front door, through the large windows, I could see the interior of the wood and mirrored art deco bar. My eye took in a few couples at the small tables, a group overcrowding a booth, and then . . . I saw dirty blond hair and a black leather jacket.

Inside, clutching my shopping bag and baguette, I made my way through the crowd toward Jacques's table, wondering if he was alone. I hadn't been able to tell through from the window. I was positive he couldn't be. After all, he wasn't there to see me. That would be magic—like Great-Grandma Berger's magic. This had to be just a coincidence. But it would be nice to say hello.

I reached the table. He was alone. There was a bottle of Champagne in an aluminum cooler. Two glasses. One empty. His half-full. Jacques looked the same. Maybe there were some more laugh lines around his eyes, but they were just as blue and just as searching as ever.

"Ciao," he said.

"Hi." I nodded.

"I saw your note."

"You did?"

"This afternoon. I was walking by the shop and something made me stop in. I realize I'm a day late, but I took a chance because I have a question . . ."

"Yes?"

"Would you like to have Champagne here"—he took a long pause—"or up in your room?"

⚜ ⚜ ⚜

*New York Times* bestselling author **M.J. Rose** grew up in New York City, mostly in the labyrinthine galleries of The Metropolitan Museum, the dark tunnels and lush gardens of Central Park, and reading her mother's favorite books before she was allowed. She is the author of more than a dozen novels; founder of the first ad agency for authors, AuthorBuzz.com; and cofounder of 1001 Dark Nights. Her latest book, *The Library of Light and Shadow*, is set in Paris and the South of France. Many of the places Jacques took her on the real-life April afternoon in this essay appear in that new novel.

### Say bonjour:

mjrose.com
Facebook: /AuthorMJRose
Pinterest: @MJRoseAuthor
Twitter: @MJRose

### The Paris Books:

*The Library of Light and Shadow*
*The Book of Lost Fragrance*
*The Seduction of Victor H.*
*The Collector of Dying Breaths*
*The Witch of Painted Sorrows*
*The Secret Language of Stones*

*I write about Paris because . . .*

I feel things more acutely in Paris. I am more aware of beauty, of smells and tastes and how things feel. I come alive there in a way I don't anywhere else in the world.

*Favorite Paris moment:*

The boat ride I took on the Seine with my mother when I was fourteen. It was our first day there. I was tired and cranky and jet-lagged and didn't want to do anything but go to sleep. But she insisted. And then the boat began its slow, sensuous trip around the city. It was *l'heure bleue* and the sky was that bluish dusk before the stars come out. and the music began playing and my mother turned to me and smiled.

She died too young, and that moment and her joy being there with me, showing me the city she loved so much, is something that stays with me always.

*Least favorite Paris moment:*

The last time I had to leave.

*In Paris, you must . . .*

Stand on any bridge at night, with the lights reflecting on the Seine, and kiss someone madly.

⚜ ⚜ ⚜

# WE'LL NEVER HAVE PARIS

*Jennifer Coburn*

Paris is often associated with romantic love. Some people imagine walking hand in hand along the River Seine with a new love, the Eiffel Tower glittering in the night sky. Others dream about an intimate candlelit dinner at a cozy bistro. For me, though, Paris has always been a city of love shared between mother and daughter.

My first trip to Paris was with my daughter, Katie, the summer after she finished second grade. She was eight years old, and as much as I loved spending time with her, there just wasn't enough of it. Katie's life was jam-packed with homework, soccer practice, art lessons, and the activities that fill the calendars of today's over-scheduled American child. As for me, I was never without a well-organized to-do list that I rarely completed, but that still gave me tremendous satisfaction when I got to check off its individual tasks. Paris seemed like an ideal mother-daughter escape.

On Katie's and my second night in Paris, we met my cousin Janine and her husband, Bruno, a native Frenchman, for dinner at their apartment overlooking the Tuileries Gardens. Bruno scanned

my map of the city, marked with different color stickers dotting places Katie and I planned to visit, and barely refrained
from rolling his eyes. He shook his head as if to say I had it all
wrong, then sipped wine from a bulbous glass and inhaled smoke
from his cigarette. Finally, in his thick accent, he said, "In order
to know Paris, you must simply relax, have a glass of wine, and
enjoy life."

Katie and I quickly tried to adopt this philosophy (minus
the wine for her). On an evening walk, we headed in the wrong
direction and stumbled upon couples dancing the tango, their
music playing on a giant boom box. Instead of rushing to correct
our course, we sat and watched the dancers as the sky behind
them dimmed from periwinkle to slate.

When we returned home to San Diego, Katie and I volleyed
Bruno's advice between us for more than a decade. Whatever
was going on at the moment, we would remind each other to
relax and enjoy life. These words were like a reset button.

Since Paris was my City of Motherly Love, I suggested a trip
with my own mother the autumn after Katie left for college. I
knew I'd be a mourning empty-nester, and as the saying goes,
Paris is always a good idea. Plus, I hadn't spent any significant
one-on-one time with my mother since I had left her nest thirty
years earlier, and the gulf between us felt wide.

I was raised almost single-handedly by my mother, who divorced my father and rented a studio apartment in Greenwich
Village in the 1970s. She enrolled me in kindergarten at the local
public school, signed me up for ballet class at the Joffrey, and
took the subway uptown to work as a news assistant at the *New*

*York Times.* Most of the time I had no idea she was struggling financially because we always seemed to be laughing.

Our upstairs neighbors were two gay guys—an opera singer and a hairdresser—who fought relentlessly. For some reason, when Opera Guy stormed out of the apartment, he never used the front door. Instead, he climbed out of their living room window and onto the fire escape. Invariably, the other would lock the window and Opera Guy would have to come downstairs to our place. He'd crawl through the window, grab our broom, and bang it on the ceiling as he shouted, continuing the fight. Life was like a sitcom without the commercial breaks.

But a lot of time had passed since our days in Greenwich Village, and my mother and I now lived on different coasts. We shared holidays and phone calls, but not the mundane intimacies of a common laundry basket or clogged plumbing. And while that is the natural order of life, it also leads to a loss of connection.

A few years ago, my mother told me she hoped my dreams would come true. When I asked her which ones, she was hard-pressed to name any. "Um, all of them," she said with a tense lilt. To be fair, I had no idea what any of her deepest hopes were, either. Sure, I knew she had attended every spiritual workshop offered, spinning her chakras, regressing through past lives, and chanting mantras. I knew she was diligent about avoiding the sunlight for fear of damaging her flawless skin, and that she was one of the handful of women who complained that she couldn't tip the scale into triple digits. And I knew that after three decades working in the Drama Department at the *Times*, she was affectionately called the Contessa of Broadway for her collection of wide-brimmed hats and gay male admirers. Beyond the fabulous character that the world saw, though, I didn't truly know my mother. I didn't know who she was at the core, what brought her the most joy, what she feared.

Visiting Paris with Katie had been the perfect way to reconnect, so I figured it would offer the same chance for my mother and me. I imagined the two of us linked at the elbows, losing track of time as we walked along the cobblestone streets sharing secrets. Cliché as this was, I longed for it. I had a fantasy that my mother, after a lifetime of pointing out great subjects for photographs, would finally pick up a camera and discover her buried artistic genius. Back home, she fought the idea, saying that squinting her eyes to use a camera would cause wrinkles. But in Paris, I hoped she would realize that at seventy-six years old, she was entitled to a few lines.

When Katie and I were in Paris, we had code words for when a situation seemed suspicious and a secret handshake for no particular reason. When we returned home, we had memories of spending the night at the Shakespeare and Company bookstore in Paris. We were nearly arrested for hopping over a playground gate at the Luxembourg Gardens. Our trip to Paris gave us inside jokes we could now exchange from across a room with a glance. I couldn't wait to experience this with my own mother.

But she declined my invitation to visit Paris together, citing the rise in anti-Semitism in France. I was deflated, but decided to cash in my frequent flyer miles and take a solo trip to Paris anyway. An empty nest was not somewhere I wanted to be, and Paris was my favorite escape.

When I told my mother about my trip, she offered to change the dates of her French river cruise and meet me in Paris for a day.

"Wait . . . you're going on a cruise through France?" I asked.

"Yes, it ends in Paris. We can spend the day together!"

"So, anti-Semitism isn't a problem as long as you're floating past it?"

"It's a senior citizen cruise where we have lectures on the boat and all of the tours and meals are taken care of," she said.

I sighed, resigning myself to the fact that I was never going to get that magical Parisian experience with my mother I had longed for. We would never wander the gardens at the Rodin museum. We would never go hat shopping and antiquing at the flea markets of Saint-Ouen. We would never sit at a sidewalk café and struggle to ask our waiter if he had anything gluten-free.

*Maybe this is all we get with our parents,* I told myself. *Maybe we never really get to know them in an intimate way. Maybe I should just be grateful for what I have with my daughter, and let go of hoping for more with my mother.* And yet it was the closeness I shared with Katie that made me feel its absence with my own mother.

Before we each left on our respective trips, she called to give me her itinerary. "They're giving us a tour of Paris, and we can either get dropped off at Notre-Dame at noon or take the tour bus back to the hotel."

"Great, let's meet at Notre-Dame," I suggested.

"No, come get me at the hotel. We'll never find each other at Notre-Dame," she said, panic rising in her voice at the thought.

"We can meet right at the front door," I suggested. "Text me when you're there."

This plan proved too stressful. "You know I don't tex!"

"Text, Mom, text. There's a *t* at the end. Tex is, like, some old oil tycoon from Houston. Anyway, there's a spot right in front called Point Zero. You can't miss it, but if you do, just ask someone."

"This is getting too complicated, Jennifer!" she said.

My mother had once specialized in complicated. Even in unfamiliar surroundings, my mother had once been fearless, some would even say reckless. In the 1980s, she was banned from Romania after exchanging money on the black market and trading Levi's and Kent cigarettes for caviar and crocheted doilies. There was a men's soccer team involved, but she's never fully shared the details. But that was a younger version, a forty-five-year-old who had no problem rendezvousing with a stranger in an alley and swapping paper bags filled with American and foreign currency. The version who took seniors cruises wasn't sure she could find the front door to Notre-Dame.

As I looked at my open suitcase on my bedroom floor, waiting to be packed and transported to Paris, I heard the familiar voice of my cousin's husband, Bruno, advising me to "Relax, have a glass of wine, and enjoy life." I mean, really, what was the big deal picking her up at her hotel? I had no problem navigating my way around the city and there was no need to insist on the most efficient plan. "Okay," I told her. "I'll come to you."

In Paris, I had three days on my own before I was to meet my mother. I thought there would be at least a few occasions when I would burst into tears remembering Katie's and my previous visit to the City of Light. Instead I visited those memories with unmitigated joy. The boy eating his Nutella crêpe with a chocolate ring around his mouth didn't gut me, but filled me with a sense of connection with his parents, who giggled as they watched him devour it. When I went to the Contemporary Art Fair at the Grand Palais, I saw a wall outside built entirely of butter. Inside among the artwork was an older couple, both bald, with theatrical makeup and fire-engine-red fur coats. I sat on the stone staircase and drank it all in, photographing the passersby in their colorful collection of scarves. I snapped shots of an enormous planter fashioned after the Incredible Hulk, surrealist paintings, and a Donald Trump piñata.

I met a lovely American woman who gave me travel tips as we shared coffee at the restaurant on top of the Musée d'Orsay. Downstairs, I caught an exhibition on prostitution, which included a black-and-white silent porno movie. Afterward, I made my way to an Andy Warhol exhibit at the Museum of Modern Art across the river. As I walked in the direction of the Eiffel Tower, sighing at how beautiful it looked with autumn foliage clinging to the trees in the foreground, I had to fight the urge to throw my cap in the air *à la* Mary Tyler Moore.

On the evening before my mother arrived in Paris, I went to a jazz club to hear a quartet whose bass player had been my seatmate on the red eye over the Atlantic Ocean. I imitated the hepcat patrons bobbing their heads to the irregular beat of the music, suppressing a smile as I had a polar variation of the same thought. First, I silently squealed self-consciously, *Holy crap, I'm sitting alone in a jazz club in Paris!* Remembering Bruno's directive to relax and enjoy life, I settled into it, feeling a bit pleased with myself. *Holy crap*, I said to myself, *I'm sitting alone in a jazz club in Paris.*

The following morning, I called my mother, who answered her phone with a dramatic *"Bonjour!"* This was her usual greeting, not one she reserved for France. She followed up with a lyrical, *"Comment allez-vous?"* Neither of us speak French, but we were in a Paris state of mind.

When I arrived at her hotel room, the door flew open and she greeted me with arms wide for an embrace. She wore a bold silk scarf and a hat that was artfully tipped to one side. Her coral lipstick slashed across her delicate white skin and she smelled like home. Some people associate their mothers with the scent of fresh-baked cookies or bread. For me, it was Arpège. *"Bonjour!"* she sang, rocking me in her embrace. *"Bonjour, bonjour, bonjour!"*

It was in moments like these that I remembered why I wanted a closer connection with my mother. Before I belonged anywhere else, she was home.

My mother mentioned that she wanted to visit the Picasso Museum before we had dinner with my cousin Janine. She and Bruno were now amicably divorced and coparenting their eleven-year-old son, Luca, the baby Katie and I had met on our first visit to Paris.

My mother looked for her missing glasses, a ritual we had been going through for my entire life. As always, they were in her purse. She asked how we would get to the Picasso Museum, so I explained that I would buy her a Métro pass for the day. "I mapped it out last night. I know exactly how to get there from here," I assured her as we left her room.

"I'll buy my ticket from the front desk of the hotel," she said as we rode down the elevator to the lobby.

"They sell them at the station; they're not going to have them at the front desk," I said.

"Sure they will," she said, her voice high with anxiety. When the hotel clerk advised her to buy her ticket at the station, she looked at me in panic. "I don't know what the hell is going on."

At the station, I bought her a ticket and fed it to the slot in the turnstile. I actually found the Paris Métro system far easier to navigate than the subways of New York, but my mother became unsettled by her lack of familiarity, and repeated that she didn't know what was going on while frantically searching for her glasses again. "Listen," I said, holding her gloved hand, "I know exactly how to get where we're going. I can either narrate the trip so you know which trains we're taking and why, or you can just trust that I'm going to get us where we need to be. I've got this covered."

She decided she wanted the blow by blow, but after a few minutes said it was overwhelming and I should just get us to the museum. I wondered when this anxiety took hold of my adventurous mother. She had been riding New York subways for nearly sixty years, so the concept of an underground train network shouldn't have been this daunting. My initial reaction was annoyance, then fear that the years were sapping the best of my mother. Of course, this made me feel guilty for my initial irritation, starting a spiral into my own anxiety. I silently resolved to be a better daughter: more patient, deferential, and conciliatory.

When we arrived at the Picasso Museum, there was a line of people snaking around the corner, but I had a special treat for her. One of the perks of working as a writer is that you can skip the line—and usually get free admission—to most museums. We approached the security guard and I flashed my press pass. Without a word, the guard nodded his head and we began walking in.

"Wait, I don't have a press pass!" my mother said too loudly.

I hushed her, reminding her that the guard was now several feet behind us. We were in. It was fine, I assured her. "But I don't have a pass. Tell him I'm your mother. Say *ma mére*, say *ma mére!*" her volume increasing and her throat tightening each time she implored me.

"Please stop talking," I whispered through gritted teeth. "Just keep walking in."

"Excuse me," said a voice from behind us. We turned to see the security guard who informed us that "zee press pass is only for zee journalist, not for *la mére.*"

I gave a pleading look. "Honestly," I told him, "she's retired from the *New York Times*. Mom, do you have an old guild card or your ID?"

"No, I have nothing. Say *ma mére!*"

*He speaks English!* I wanted to scream. *You're standing right here listening to him speak English and he can hear you shouting* 'ma mére'! *It doesn't seem to be impressing him.*

So much for my resolution to be a good daughter.

If this were a movie, Bruno's words would pipe in as voice-over, reminding me to "Relax, have a glass of wine, and enjoy life." I took a breath and looked at the security guard and scrunched my face in an expression that begged for his help. In a moment, we seemed to have a silent exchange that went like this:

*Me: Do you have a mother?*

*Him: Say no more. They are crazy, but we must love them.*

"Okay, you go," the guard said, nodding us in.

As we walked through the doors of the museum, my mother gave me a gentle poke with her elbow. "See, just tell people *ma mére* and they help. They're anti-Semites, but they do love their mothers." Her relief lasted only a moment as she saw another set of security guards. "Oh no!" she yelped too loudly. "More guards, and I don't have a ticket."

"Mom, please!" I snapped. "We are in—please stop drawing attention to us by saying that in front of every guard we see. At this point, they just want to make sure we don't steal a painting."

Why did this woman refuse to relax and enjoy life? Was it even a choice for her? Was this where I was headed?

Cementing my anxiety was my mother's familiar refrain. "I don't know what the hell is going on," she said, then stopped in front of a sculpture of a goat Katie had sketched ten years earlier. I have a photo of my daughter wearing a pink beret and a focused expression as she held her yellow school pencil over her sketch pad. I smiled at the memory before hearing my mother's voice across the room. "I think Picasso hated women," she said, standing in front of a Cubist painting. "Look how she's all chopped up. That's not someone who likes women."

After we had our fill of Picasso, it was time to head to Janine's new apartment near Luxembourg Gardens. First we would have to make our way back to the Métro station, which meant a nice stroll through Le Marais. As we exited the museum, I saw my mother open her mouth to speak, but cut her off. "I know exactly what the hell is going on," I assured her. "Come on, *ma mére*, let's go listen to that street performer. I think she's singing '*La Vie en Rose*.'"

As we joined the crowd of people listening, I reminded myself that a good daughter was patient and kind, especially when her mother grew older. *I am calm and patient*, I repeated to myself silently. *Unlock your jaw and unclench your butt cheeks.*

Soon after, we were at Janine's home drinking tea and watching clips from her upcoming documentary on Syria. Bruno no longer lived there, so I didn't expect to see him, but was pleasantly surprised when I heard his voice making its way through the foyer and into Janine's kitchen. He looked similar to when I had met him a decade ago—three-day razor stubble, a leather coat, and an air of indifference. Still, his message to relax, have a glass of wine, and enjoy life had made him somewhat of a Messiah in my life.

"This is my aunt Carol," Janine told Bruno. "And you remember Jennifer."

He politely greeted us. "It is a pleasure to meet you," Bruno said.

*Meet me?!* I gasped internally. *Did he just say it was a pleasure to . . .*

"Oh, you've met Jennifer," my mother piped in. Great, furthering the humiliation of being completely forgotten was my mother reminding him that he, in fact, forgot he'd met me.

"Well, it was a long time ago," I said, feigning nonchalance.

"Oh, but you said something that really stuck with Jennifer, didn't he?" my mother said, her head going back and forth between us.

*Yeah, it's been the guiding principle of my existence for the last decade, but whatever. Nice to meet you, too.*

My mother kept that conversation going in a way only a mother could. It was clear Bruno had no interest in what he'd said that impressed me. He just wanted to pick up Luca and be on his way. "Tell Bruno what he said, Jennifer," my mother coaxed. Then, to my great mortification, she promised, "It will only take two seconds."

Now all heads were turned to me. "Oh, you just said that in order to know Paris, you need to simply relax, have a glass of wine, and enjoy life."

Silence hung in their air for a few moments. Bruno made a face as if to say that this comment sounded like him. "Well, did you do eet?" I nodded. "Good. Then you keep doing eet." It wasn't the Sermon on the Mount, but it would have to do.

Walking back to the Métro station, I told my mother I felt disappointed that Bruno didn't even remember meeting me. "I know we all meet a ton of people and a lot of time has gone by, but *nice to meet you?* Janine even reminded him that we'd already met."

We descended into the Métro station and did the ritual peek down the tunnel to see if we could spot the headlight from the train. "Why does it matter?" she asked.

"I mean, here's this person whose words changed my entire worldview, and I was so insignificant to him that he didn't even recall that we'd ever even met," I explained. "I just find it depressing."

The train arrived and we got on, finding two seats next to each other. My mother placed her purse on her lap and turned to me. "I think it's wonderful," she said. "If someone could be such a source of inspiration to another and not even have it register with them, that might mean we're all walking around having a transformative impact on other people all the time, every day, and have absolutely no idea. Imagine the possibilities."

"Wow, that's some good stuff, *ma mère*. And you say you don't know what the hell is going on," I said.

"I still don't know where this train is going," she said, her tone returning to its familiar anxiety. "And I think I left my glasses at Janine's."

❧

After my mother and I returned to the United States, I spent some time with her in New York. She had moved to the city when she was nineteen years old and never left, saying that nowhere else in the world could compare to the culture and excitement of Manhattan. She loves it just as much in her retirement, but unquestionably regarded her single life in the late 1950s and '60s in Greenwich Village as the best years of her life. She was a student at NYU and lived with two women who had a strict code of never venturing north of Fourteenth Street or paying more than a few dollars for theater tickets. They volunteered at the Provincetown Playhouse on MacDougal Street, where they caught the first run of Edward Albee's *The Zoo Story* and Samuel Beckett's *Krapp's Last Tape.*

"Why don't we go for a walk in the Village?" I asked, knowing this was one of her favorite things to do. "You can tell me about the olden days."

Walking tours of her youth were one of her favorite activities, though they were bittersweet because most of her old haunts were gone. Cheap bohemian hideouts had become trendy hipster bars. Tenements where artists once lived had been converted to lofts for hedge fund managers. Still, there were enough relics of disappearing New York to scavenge.

Our walk began where it always did: Sheridan Square, at the apartment she had shared with two girlfriends who wore flannel shirts and cropped hair. Pointing up at the redbrick building, she gestured to her bedroom window. "I ran to school, then ballet class, then we went out at night," she said, the memory close. "We were never tired and we were never bored."

We crossed the street and passed the Stonewall Inn, the historic bar where the riots of 1969 largely sparked the modern gay rights movement. "I never knew it was a gay bar. It wasn't like it is today with the pink neon sign and rainbow flag outside. I walked past here every day and I'd see guys coming and going and I never had any idea what this place would come to mean someday."

"Too bad you didn't know," I said. "You'd have made a lot of new friends." We turned a corner and headed down a street with a canopy of old trees and brownstones with generous picture windows.

"I had no shortage of friends," she scoffed. "Being gay was a big secret back then, so I'd go to all of the office parties with my male friends who passed me off as their girlfriend." With a spring in her voice, she told me, "I was the most popular beard in the Village."

In Paris, she felt lost, but in Greenwich Village, my mother definitely knew what the hell was going on, and the familiarity was a relief for both of us. For her, because she was in her element. For me, because I wasn't carrying the weight of her discomfort.

She enjoyed spotting Village institutions that had survived gentrification. An Italian meat market. A hardware store. The historic redbrick Jefferson Market Library with its storybook clock tower. My mother pointed out Norman Mailer's old apartment that he shared with his wife. "Good God, could those two fight!" she recalled. The shouting would sweep the entire block.

More difficult for my mother was remembering what places used to be. "This was a hole-in-the-wall mom-and-pop sandwich shop." She pointed at a vegan lunch spot. "And this was a great little boutique where I bought a red belted wool jacket and matching hat," she said, then thought twice about it. "Or maybe that was where Duane Reade was." The transformation of the neighborhood forced us to take note of the change in ourselves, and the past always looked a little better. As a child, I remember complaining about the garbage on the streets, the smell of urine, and the sight of graffiti on the subways. As memories, though, these were signs of vitality. Of *real* New York.

As we turned another corner and made our way down a curved street of old carriage houses, my mother told me about the time her friends entered her in a drag contest. "Larry told me to put on my black pants and my black turtleneck, and I didn't give it a second thought. They were always telling me what to wear," she recalled with a laugh. "They entered me as a man dressed as a woman. I had a real gamine look back then, so John slicked back my hair, and *voilà*!"

"Did you know they were entering you in a drag contest?" I asked.

"Not at first," she said. "I came in second place. This drag queen was all dolled up with a sequined evening gown and a tiara. No one stood a chance."

We continued our walk, heading for Washington Square Park. When we made it to the Arc de Triomphe of New York, the arch in Washington Square Park, my mother needed to sit, so we grabbed a spot on a bench overlooking the fountain where children would splash in the summer months. The NYU campus enveloped the park, its purple canopies and signs staking their claim in the bustling neighborhood.

My mother's eyes scanned the park, watching the musicians and drug dealers, ever-present like human mist. Students busily darted to their next destination and tourists walked tentatively with their maps. "I have no idea where the time went," my mother said. "Half the people I knew are dead and I'm afraid I'll be the last one standing." She looked at me, and continued with a calm that belied her words. "I've been a seeker my entire life, but don't feel like I'm complete yet."

I wanted to tell her that she was already complete, but assurances like these, no matter how well intended, deny a person their emotional truth. She was facing the hard realities of aging: witnessing a changing world, accepting physical limitations, watching friends die, and questioning the meaning of her own life. That was not something that could be patched over with cheerful promises from me.

"That must be rough," I said.

"It's a challenge," she replied.

It was as close as she'd ever let me in, and I longed for more. But my mother is a master of the emotional pivot, and that was all I got.

"Did I tell you about the little tiff I'm having with the director of my scene from *The Crucible*?" she asked with a mischievous smile. In her retirement, my mother was taking daily classes at an organization for lifelong learners, a euphemism for seniors. The acting classes were among her favorite. Last season, she was cast as a streetwalker in a Southern drama, but insisted that they modify the role because who would believe *she* was a hooker? The role was changed to a high-priced call girl. Now she was fighting for *The Crucible*'s Elizabeth Proctor to wear lipstick onstage.

"Wasn't Elizabeth Proctor a Quaker?" I asked.

"A Quaker who would've looked a lot better with a little lipstick," she said. "I'm wearing that awful bonnet. This is the least they can do."

When Katie and I returned from our mother-daughter trip to Paris, I borrowed a line from *Casablanca* and told her we'd always have Paris. My mother and I, we'd never have Paris. We'd never share stories about sleeping at the Shakespeare and Company bookstore like Katie and I did. We would never have memories of exploring Montmartre. We wouldn't even have a photo of ourselves in front of the Eiffel Tower.

What we did have, though, was a start. I knew more about my mother than I ever had after our walk together through Greenwich Village. I told her I wanted more. More time. More space to let the relationship deepen. It went without saying that our time together wouldn't last forever, and I didn't want it to end with my feeling I only knew my mother as well as the next person.

"What do you want to know?" she asked, then started listing her character traits.

"I don't want your résumé," I said. "I want to spend unhurried time together and see who you are rather than hearing bullet points."

She sighed audibly, giving it some thought. "Okay," she said. "We can do that."

Knowing she was willing to try filled my heart with hope and my eyes with tears. A moment passed. I giggled at a thought. "You know what this means we're going to be doing, Mom?"

She raised an eyebrow, coaxing me to continue.

"We're going to take Bruno's advice and relax, have a glass of wine, and enjoy life," I said.

"Can we make it herbal tea? Wine turns straight to sugar

when it hits your system, and nothing causes inflammation like sugar," she said.

I smiled. "Okay, *ma mére,* herbal tea it is.*"

⚜ ⚜ ⚜

**Jennifer Coburn** is the *USA Today* bestselling author of six novels and the mother-daughter travel memoir *We'll Always Have Paris.* She is also an award-winning journalist who has written for dozens of national and regional publications, including *Mothering, The Washington Post,* the *Miami Herald, The San Diego Union-Tribune, Salon,* and *The Huffington Post.* When she's not working, Jennifer is reading, going to the theater, or overindulging in good food.

Jennifer lives in San Diego with her husband, William.

### Say bonjour:
jennifercoburn.com
Facebook: /JenniferCoburnBooks
Twitter: @JenniferCoburn
Instagram: @JenniferCoburnBooks

### The Paris Book:
*We'll Always Have Paris*

### Favorite Paris moment:
I attended a chocolate fashion show in Paris last fall at the Salon du Chocolat and was astounded by the

artistry of the gowns and accessories made entirely of chocolate. It was absolutely breathtaking, but what really struck me was when a musician dropped the bow of her violin during the opening performance. My heart skipped a beat, terrified for her, but she was completely unfazed. She made a graceful movement and reached down to the stage floor, sweeping up her bow as if it were all part of the show.

### Least favorite Paris moment:

When my daughter, Katie, was eight years old, we slept at the Shakespeare and Company bookstore on the Left Bank. My daughter had a wonderful attitude, noticing only our perfect view of Notre-Dame Cathedral. I took in the smell of hot garbage from the street below and thought our room should have been condemned. Henry Miller had slept there, and it looked like that was the last time they had changed the sheets. Katie's bed was a yoga mat covering a door that rested on top of two file cabinets (of unequal height). When I turned on the faucet, water did not come out, but a tornado of gnats did. And in the corner was a box of Ritz Crackers with a picture of a very youthful Andy Griffith. When I woke up the next morning, three little mouse turds were next to my pillow. More than a decade later, I still can't think of that room without quivering. Katie thought it was absolutely wonderful.

***In Paris, you must . . .***

I went to an English-language dinner party at an expat's apartment in the 14th arrondissement. Jim Haynes has been hosting open-house feasts most Sunday nights for more than thirty-five years. Guests pay a flat fee of around 35 euros and get wonderful food, wine—and great conversation. I met travelers from around the world and native Parisians like Edith de Belleville, who give tours off the beaten path, like the brothels of the Marais and lovers of Paris.

⚜ ⚜ ⚜

# READING PARIS

## *Cathy Kelly*

Being fourteen means living with a howling ache of confusion. Of feeling lost and misunderstood, of being in two worlds and not belonging in either.

Now, at fifty, I understand that at fourteen, plenty of people felt out of step but that nobody talked about it—we were all desperately trying to belong. Yet inside, we felt different. Some of us wrote bad poetry to help ourselves out of it, but take it from me: Bad poetry never helps.

If I were fourteen now, I would have an entire genre of young adult books to help me celebrate this difference. Books where being different is good, means being able to shoot fire from your fingertips, send an arrow flying from your bow, save the world.

But thirty-six years ago, there were fewer books on being out of step—apart from Judy Blume—and no advice on using mindfulness to survive teenage angst, no mention of how a gratitude diary can actually help, how this too shall pass.

I had read Oscar Wilde's famous phrase: "Be yourself. Everybody else is taken."

But really? *Be yourself*? Pure madness. Myself was hopeless. How could I ever exist by being myself?

In my search for how to cope with being different and actually live, I turned to books—something I have done all my life. If in need of information, read a book on it. I am the woman who brought three books into the hospital when I was ready to give birth to twins. As backup.

Since I was three and first brought to the library, I had been systematically going through the children's canon. I was Jo in *Little Women* and thought of writing in a garret like her, but really, what a silly idea, I told myself. How could *I* write?

But I loved losing myself in the stories. I could almost taste the maple tree sap from Laura Ingalls Wilder's *Little House in the Big Woods*, and would honestly never quite forgive Scarlett for not making it right with Rhett. I'm not sure I ever forgave Amy for taking Laurie away from Jo, either. Even now, when I watch the film versions, I still squint a little at Amy. How could she?

At the age of twelve, I was allowed to join the adult library— three years early—as I had read all the kids' books, and besides, I had been checking out adult books on my mother's card for about a year.

Released officially into this adult world, I became an Agatha Christie junkie, devoured the vast historical novels of English kings and queens by Jean Plaidy, read Colleen McCullough's *The Thorn Birds* in total secrecy (aged eleven and three-quarters, after I had been forbidden to), and dallied briefly with the stories of Angelique by Anne Golon, a series that started in 1957 and involved a heroine from seventeenth-century France who has the worst luck of any woman, ever. Angelique was forever being captured and carried off by men whom she either fought or fell in love with. If that girl had had a passport, it would have been full of stamps.

A friend's mother was a fan of Barbara Cartland novels and once, on holiday with their family, I read several. As a writer, Barbara was a big fan of ellipses. Heroines fell against dukes (always dukes) and fluttered their tiny hands and then he'd stare at her and kiss her and . . .

I started reading spy novels, which I still love, and devastatingly tragic books about the Warsaw ghetto in the Second World War, and novels of huge pain of Irish people fleeing the Famine on ships to America. They were called coffin ships because so many people died on them.

But it was *The Three Musketeers* that led me to Paris. I didn't know why that particular book flicked a switch that day when I was fourteen.

Now I know that, as with all books, it was simply the right book in the right place at the right time. As a writer who has published eighteen books, when people come up to me and say, "This one of your books is my favorite," I will know that it was the right book in the right place at the right time to make life seem better, more hopeful.

On the morning of the day I discovered Dumas, I had been feeling ill and didn't want to go to school, but *I had no books left. Crisis!* So I went into school, went straight to the library, picked up the Musketeers, and then announced that I was sick and had to go home.

There was something about the filmy pages of that old,

red-backed novel with its tooled spine, and the sense that nobody had picked it up for many years. I was no longer an Irish girl in bed—I was in the noisy, dirty city of Paris with its glorious architecture, teeming with life and excitement and . . . difference.

Ireland in those years, despite our rich cultural heritage, had few exquisite buildings because so many had been taken, burned down, allowed to decay. There were no streets—although there should have been—like the streets of Dumas's Paris, where wooden houses and great stone mansions stood cheek by jowl, where around every corner, there was another honeyed stone monument to architecture, wealth, and empire. It was totally different from Paris.

Yet this difference was accessible because of the people, the real feelings of the people within his stories: The queen, cloistered in danger because in those days, to be royal in any country was to watch your back. Athos, noble scion, shattered by love. D'Artagnan, poor country boy on a clodhopper of a horse, yet filled with the dreams of what he could become. Porthos, always broke.

As a writer, I fall in love in every sense with people, and Dumas's characters struck a chord with me—despite the different centuries, the different location, the vast differences between a young teenager in a Dublin suburb snuggled in her bed, grateful to be missing school for this blissful respite and the people she met on those pages, and the Musketeers, fighting for love, and honor, and justice.

For most people, *The Three Musketeers* was a rollicking adventure, probably a boys' book, ripe for bad screen adaptations. But for me, it was an introduction into another world—of corruption, spying, and dying for what you believe in.

Set in France in 1625, it was a world where scheming cardinals and exquisite miladies with the fleur-de-lis, the mark of a thief, branded on them, destroyed noble men like Athos and nearly upset the entire world.

Like Victor Hugo, Dumas shows the poverty and unfairness of life. There were the highborn people and the poor ones, who owed money for rent, who must bow to the miladies and suffer the indignities of being a peasant.

While other, lesser Musketeer-lovers adored the youthful D'Artagnan and his battle for acceptance in this world of the king's guards, I loved Athos nearly more than I loved Rhett Butler, and that was saying something. Rhett and Athos were both wounded by love, but Rhett would recover, whereas Athos never would. His heart had been too badly damaged. He would simply never be the same again.

And Paris, this city, captured my heart. I was like the seventeen-year-old D'Artagnan, who came into the city on his old farm horse, full of hope and excitement, ready to start a new life.

I was probably too mature in many ways, thought too much, certainly worried too much, and could not imagine having the courage to race off to Paris like D'Artagnan. But his city was not just beautiful: it was a community. People jostled friends, women chattered on the streets, Porthos couldn't walk along a street without meeting at least four people he owed money to. The sense of *fraternité* that became a rallying cry for the French Revolution was in the air.

There began my love affair with Paris, and it has never stopped.

I have four editions of *The Three Musketeers*—I am always

searching for a volume with filmier paper, like that first beloved one where turning each page was like a whisper.

I kept barreling through books and belonged to three libraries at this point, not including the school one. That was also the summer I read *Valley of the Dolls* and much of the Harold Robbins canon—the girls-only convent school library had been gifted many books, and since nobody but me ever went in there, nobody saw Robbins sitting there. (When the head nun saw me carrying a Daphne du Maurier novel once, and smiled and said they were a little immoral, I knew then that she had never seen the Robbins shelf.)

Soon after, my parents noticed a thriller with vivid sex scenes (which I swear wasn't why I was reading it) idly left on the mantelpiece. It was a school library book. They marched into the head nun's office and the library was de-sexed.

At fifteen, I read Voltaire's *Candide* while babysitting, instead of looking through my hosts' record collection, which was what everyone else who babysat seemed to do.

I consumed *Bonjour Tristesse*, an often overlooked novel by Françoise Sagan featuring a seventeen-year-old, Cecile, who was worldly and sophisticated compared to my own then sixteen-year-old self, chock-full of anxieties and utterly lacking in any elegance or *soigneé*-ness. Cecile lived in Paris and had cool clothes and could flirt. I had no cool clothes, had no reason to flirt, and lived in a Dublin suburb where there were fabulous guys but none of them looked at me, except perhaps as a good scorekeeper for rounders, as I was such a hopeless catcher.

And yet I could understand Cecile's story. As with my

Musketeers, the differences in our lives and the times we lived in didn't matter. Life, it appeared, was re-created and repeated all the time. Friendships, loves, fears, insecurities: All these things bypass the differences in our actual corporeal lives.

I had two lives as a reader—my own, and the lives and worlds I could inhabit via books. There was always something in them that made me feel that I was not alone. With a book, as I was later to discover when I started writing professionally myself, it didn't matter where you set it or when. People would understand.

In school, in the higher French class, we dutifully translated Sartre into English. *La Nausée.* Nausea. His first novel was full of existential angst that we didn't understand. But we weren't supposed to understand it, I think—just know how to translate it.

We might have had a better chance of understanding or connecting if someone had given us a few philosophy classes or told us about Simone de Beauvoir and their love. Or imagine if someone had quoted de Beauvoir herself: *"On ne naît pas femme, on le deviant."* "One is not born a woman, one becomes one."

But we knew nothing of the private lives of the writers we translated. No details about how the Irish geniuses James Joyce and Samuel Beckett had loved France; how Henry Miller and Anaïs Nin loved each other; and how in the Paris of the Roaring Twenties, everyone who was everyone came to share in the intellectual and social whirl.

No, we translated Sartre as if we were translating bistro menus—"Is that *with* mushrooms or without?"—and nobody ever spoke to us in the language properly, until the French *assistant*, who was drafted in one summer term because he was actually French and it was thought that might help with our pronunciation.

Christian turned up when I was in my final year in school, by this time cloaked in a navy sweater. (In sixth year, we were allowed wear a navy sweater rather than the wire wool royal blue version we'd worn for the previous five years, a garment that rasped our skin off more successfully than any pumice stone. We were also allowed to wear a white shirt, which was better for the complexion that the cream one we'd worn till then, a color that made all but the most olive-complexioned look as if they were off to a plague hospital any moment.)

We all stared dreamily at Christian until the nuns, sensing danger, decided that it was too late to teach us French with an actual French person and flung him into the junior classes in case we overthrew him, pinned him to the floor, and asked why were French girls so cool, and why don't French women get fat? Surely a whole nation of women can't stop themselves from standing at the kitchen counter stuffing chocolate brioche into their mouths when they are either premenstrual or else miserable? And the scarf-tying? Were there lessons? We needed to know.

But we never got the answers to our questions, and I don't think we learned to pronounce anything any better. Still, I thought I was quite good at French, until I hit college and we were played actual French radio in the French journalism class and asked to translate it. Several of us nearly died from shock. Was this actual French? It was so fast! What were they saying? Was it being played at the correct speed or was it a weird patois?

Alas, it seemed that I might speak French beautifully to an Irish person who spoke back slowly, but was no good in the cut and thrust of rapid-fire native French delivery.

But I wouldn't be defeated by any inconvenient realities. I read on—meeting Colette when I was eighteen. She wrote the perfect novel—*Chéri*: read it and see if I am wrong. The beautiful Leá is an aging courtesan who takes on a friend's twenty-year-old son to knock him into shape and falls in love with him: so bittersweet and so beautiful.

He must leave and he does. The white-skinned Leá, who wears her pearls to bed and deserves happiness, knows that life is not always simple and that we must sometimes let our dreams go.

I read everything Colette had ever written.

I could see Mme. Colette on the Riviera, white sands against narrow brown feet slid into perfect espadrilles, lean men languidly standing beside her as they contemplated their existence, all smoking Gauloises.

⚜

I got to Paris—the real Paris—in the end, many times. I needed to see the Louvre and its many incarnations, from the early days to when Marie Antoinette lived there. I needed to walk over the Pont Neuf, the first Parisian bridge without houses on it, built just before the time in which *The Three Musketeers* was set. I wanted to wander the Marais and the cultural haunts of de Beauvoir, Sartre, and Beckett, see the legendary bookshop Shakespeare and Company, wander in Les Tuileries, where so many people had walked in so many of the books I read.

I spent two days in the Louvre, avoiding the queues at *La Gioconda* because why battle the crowds as if there was only one painting in the building when there were a million? But in those long, long corridors, sometimes I looked out at the windows at another side of the huge onetime palace and thought of all the machinations I'd read about that had gone on in this place in another time, and how many of those who'd lived here had died so horribly.

La Musée d'Orsay kept me busy for another day, and I had to be hauled out, then to drift down any small road to find a café where someone sat at a bar, drinking *pastis* or *un café*, watching the world, nodding, ready to talk or perhaps flirt, or make pictures with their hands the way French people do. If Irish people speak with our hands, the population of France performs opera with theirs.

The parks reminded me of Leá's drives with her young lover in Colette's *Chéri*, knowing he was leaving. You see so many shops in Paris showing rich old pearls, gleaming but waiting for the life to be breathed back into them, which Colette tells us can only happen when they are worn.

Just to walk along the Seine, traverse the bridges, stare at the Palais Royal—once the palace of Cardinal Richelieu, the bad guy in Dumas's *The Three Musketeers*. Seeing that magnificent building, an exquisite creation of power and wealth, claimed by that dastardly man, was like being in the Musketeers' world.

Last year, we gave up on an ill-fated attempt at "glamping" after five days of rain and raced up to Paris on the train, and found a little apartment with a large penthouse balcony from which you could see Sacré-Coeur. We could sit on our balcony looking at all these beautiful Parisian roofs and see people inside, living, laughing, making coffee, and racing out their doors to their busy lives.

We could plan our days depending on whether we wanted to walk or meander, shop or race through the Louvre as if it would never let us inside again. I always feel that in Paris: that this is my last visit and I must cram everything in. I must see every bit of the city I had read about for so many years.

But I know I will come back to the City of Light because she does something to me, lights me up like the glittering lights on the Eiffel Tower, which really gives you a thigh workout if you forfeit the lifts, I can tell you.

Maybe we do live other lives before these. I know, a not always popular concept, and particularly in a country where Catholicism has not had a section of reincarnation installed. But I do feel that some places speak to us. Paris speaks to me. It has always spoken to me, ever since I sat in my bed with *The Three Musketeers* that day, as a confused fourteen-year-old. And I keep speaking back.

⚜ ⚜ ⚜

**Cathy Kelly** is a *Sunday Times* and international bestselling author from Ireland. She has written over eighteen books, which have been translated into many languages. A former journalist, she lives in County Wicklow, Ireland, with her husband, their twin sons, and three Jack

Russell dogs—who are entirely in charge. She has been an Ambassador for UNICEF Ireland since 2005.

**Say bonjour:**
> cathykelly.com
> Twitter: @cathykellybooks

**The Paris Book:**
> *It Started With Paris*

**Favorite Paris moment:**
> Taking my sons to Paris the first time was quite magical, as I'd talked so much about it. Plus, they both love art and we were staying in this glorious teeny apart-hotel with a balcony near Montmartre, where you could look over the rooftops, drink your coffee, and pretend you were Parisian. We spent hours in the Louvre, in all the museums, had a go on the Ferris wheel in the Tuileries (I am scared of heights and the blasted thing went round three times . . .), and ate in tiny cafés.

**Least favorite Paris moment:**
> As a former journalist, I wrote a lot of gritty stories and worked in some gritty areas—getting lost in the Porte de Clichy area and genuinely being followed by cars who thought we were hookers was no fun. I have interviewed a lot of working women; it's such a horrendous way to have to make money, and my heart goes out to them.

**_Favorite book about Paris:_**

I love Simone de Beauvoir's _Memoirs of a Dutiful Daughter_ because she describes Paris so wonderfully.

**_Song that reminds you of Paris:_**

One of my favorite albums is from a hysterical Billy Crystal and Debra Winger movie called _Forget Paris_, the soundtrack of which I got when I was a film reviewer. I have written some part of all my books to this soundtrack. Yeah, that does sound obsessed . . .

**_Favorite non-Paris travel destination:_**

A place in Ireland called Ardmore in County Waterford, where the Man Booker Prize–winning novelist Molly Keane lived. It's on a rocky bit of coast, has an ancient holy well dating to well before Christianity, a pilgrim walk around the cliff-head, plus a beautiful hotel called the Cliff House, which perches on the rocks and from which you can watch the waves exploding into white froth beneath you. It's truly magical and gives you the sense that if time ever fractures, it would be here—where you could sneak into another world.

⚜ ⚜ ⚜

# FINDING PARIS'S HIDDEN PAST

*Rachel Hore*

One cold and rainy holiday in that odd limbo between Christmas and New Year, I was beguiled into setting a novel in Paris. I was visiting the city with my family—my husband and three teenage sons—at the end of 2012. We had rented a small apartment overlooking the rue du Temple in that part of the city whose name, Le Marais, refers to its long-ago marshy origins, but which now, with its bijoux shops and delicatessens, is a home to smart bohemians.

It's well known that teenagers inhabit different time zones from their parents. While I was up and breakfasted by nine each morning, ready to set out into the drizzle to explore the classics of modern art in the inside-out Georges Pompidou Center, or to view the city from the top of Napoleon's Arc de Triomphe, my three boys, like vampires, having stayed up half the night watching television, refused to be woken until lunchtime, when the daylight was already waning. In addition, I lost my one supporter, for my husband contracted a fluey cold. One morning, I found myself setting out to wander the streets alone. As a mother, I was disappointed, but as a writer, this turned out to be the best possible thing that could have happened.

Paris is known as the City of Light because of its love of pleasure and gaiety, and its vibrant nightlife, but also for the lights of its bridges reflecting softly off the narrow river, and for the pearly gray stone of its buildings. That day, however, with the rain rushing in cataracts along the gloomy winter streets, it didn't live up to its name. Instead, I saw another side of it revealed, something dark that lurked beneath the elegant surface. I saw its history of suffering and violence.

Around many a street corner, on the side of a bridge or at the base of a fountain or the plinth of a statue, I came across inscriptions memorializing some past war or popular struggle. The column on Place de la Bastille, near Le Marais, commemorates the 1,800 people who were killed in the July Revolution of 1830. The place itself is the site of the old Bastille prison, symbol of France's oppressive monarchy, the *ancien régime*. The Bastille was stormed by rebels on July 14, 1789, now France's national day, triggering the French Revolution. Of more recent vintage, I found reminders of World War II, when Paris was occupied by Nazi forces for more than four years.

One afternoon during our stay, this time accompanied by our boys (all vampires love a graveyard), we strolled through the labyrinthine Père Lachaise cemetery in eastern Paris, stopping from time to time to pay homage at the graves of the famous: Frédéric Chopin, Colette, Gertrude Stein, Alice B. Toklas, Oscar Wilde, and Doors guitarist Jim Morrison, the founding member of the 27 Club, whose premature death in 1971 from a drug overdose is still remembered by mourners, who leave graffiti, lit candles, and flowers on his tombstone. Eventually we came to a broad avenue, lined with war memorials under the trees. Here were cenotaphs to the victims of Nazi concentration camps, to martyred Resistance fighters, to the dead of all the different Allied armies who helped liberate France in 1944.

Passing all these somber tableaux commemorating the glorious dead forced me to consider what it might have been like to inhabit a city that lay helpless under the might of a brutal foreign power. From this moment, my imagination began to work. An idea for a novel had begun to unfold in my mind.

After that point, the city started to look different to me. It wasn't its current shape that I needed to see as much as how it had been in the past.

The greatest challenge for me as a writer of historical fiction was to find ways in which I could actually get under the skin of the city, to be able to imagine what it was like to live there in those troubled years. I was able to gather a great deal from diaries, memoirs, and films of the time. At one point I remember endlessly replaying a sequence of a film taken at a rail station during the war, trying to work out exactly where the doors on the train carriages were and how they opened. Small details, you might think, but the authenticity of a whole dramatic scene about the separation of a child from its mother was dependent upon me getting this little bit right.

One of my characters was to be a fictional American doctor working at the real-life American hospital in Neuilly, in western Paris, and among the books I consulted was the useful *Americans in Paris* by Charles Glass, which examines the stories of many different individuals who, for a variety of reasons, remained in the city during the war. It opens with the author discovering an important memorial that I had missed in my own perambulations. It is on a huge fountain in the Place Saint-Michel by the Seine in the Latin Quarter, and dedicated to those who endured the occupation of the city by German forces. It was all too easy for me to have missed it on that first visit because of the traffic rushing past it, but on a subsequent trek to the city I took care to search it out. Seeing the memorial moved me so much I became determined to honor the bravery of these people in my writing.

My second visit took place in July, a year and a half after that rainy post-Christmas holiday. This time I was accompanied only by my eldest son, a studious boy of twenty-one, about to embark on an MA in English literature, and a little better at rising in the mornings than he had been eighteen months before. Sometimes, we met partway through the day and explored places where we both wanted to go. One day we went to see Monet's water lilies in the Jeu de Paume, to bathe in the colored light from those huge, extraordinary, calming paintings, an experience I gave to Fay, a character in my novel *A Week in Paris*. Afterward, we enjoyed lunch together in a typical sidewalk café on a street missed by most tourists, behind the rue de Rivoli. Then I left him reading Proust in a deck chair in the sunny Tuileries Gardens while I went off to hunt alone for the past.

This research trip was vitally important, because by now I'd completed a first draft of my novel. Now I needed to walk the streets as my characters had done, to take notes and photographs in order to be able to breathe further life into the fictional world that I had created from real historical events. I had created my central character, Kitty, but now I had to convey convincingly her experience of fleeing Paris in early June 1940, then of being forced to return in the face of the approaching enemy forces. I had to imagine what it would have been like for her to carry her infant daughter through the deserted city that lay open and defenseless to the German advance.

Memoirs told me about the sound of explosions as the retreating French soldiers blew up the city's arsenals. Several diaries remark on the spectacular blueness of the sky during those days. Then there are many descriptions of the sheer overwhelming weight of vehicles and numbers of German soldiers that marched into the city on the 14th, but I wanted to stand at the point where Kitty might have in order to gauge which streets and which buildings draped with swastika flags she might have been able to view as she watched them arrive. And following her trajectory this way, with the help of a 1938 guidebook, I discovered a Paris I hadn't experienced before, a Paris seen through the filter of my imagination of the past.

Given that so many of its people suffered and died at the hands of the occupying forces, it is ironic that the fabric of the city itself was not destroyed. It was fascinating to read why it survived and to find what a close call it had been. On June 13, 1940, the American ambassador William Christian Bullitt Jr., whom the departing French government had left as a temporary mayor of the city the day before, assured the German army commanders that Paris would be open to them—that is, in return for peaceful occupation, the citizens would not resist. And so it happened.

Four years later, as the Allied forces surrounded Paris and its citizens rose in revolt against its Nazi occupiers, Hitler ordered that the city be razed to the ground. Explosives were planted under every bridge and power station and water-pumping plant, as well as under the most famous monuments: the Eiffel Tower, the Louvre, Les Invalides with Napoleon's tomb. But the general in charge, Dietrich von Choltitz, hoping to calm the uprising, delayed executing the Führer's orders, and after that, events overtook him. And so the city itself was spared. With this knowledge, I found that the center of Paris I had wandered around in 2014 was pretty much the same place as it was in my 1938 guidebook. To think how many of those wonderful buildings were heartbeats from destruction still makes me shiver.

Inevitably some things about the city have changed. My heroine, Kitty, practiced the piano in the Conservatoire, the national college of music. It's in the unassuming-looking rue de Madrid near the Gare Saint-Lazare, but when I visited, I was thrown off balance to see that its entrance had been modernized, all glass and metal and sliding doors, whereas I had imagined for my novel a poky old hall with a porter's desk and wooden pigeonholes and a dreaming courtyard beyond. I stood outside in the street watching the streams of students coming in and out, all dressed in jeans and Converse and printed scarves, and tried to visualize my graceful Kitty passing among them in her elegant frock and hat and gloves, her music tucked under her arm. It was too difficult, and I turned away with a heavy heart.

I had more luck walking back toward the main street, where a host of small piano and violin shops lay waiting for me to explore. In the novel, Kitty's American doctor fiancé, Eugene, visited such a shop in 1938 to acquire a piano to give her as a wedding present. I was drawn into an atelier that was crammed with stringed instruments and spare parts from floor to ceiling, and across the ceiling, too! It felt as though it had been like that for centuries, and though not strictly relevant to my story, I appreciated this atmosphere of the past.

A frequent problem in my research was gauging physical distance. It's a trick of the memory for us to think that places we've visited are closer to one another than they actually are. Occasionally, this error could affect the timing in a scene. I needed, for instance, to test the walk from the Conservatoire to Saint-Germain, on the other side of the river, which is where I imagined Kitty and Eugene to have lived in an apartment high above the street, where from the window they could see swallows dip and dive for insects. At one point, Kitty needed to rush home at short notice. How long would it have taken her? The answer was, longer than I'd thought, much longer, and I was quite out of breath by the time I arrived at my destination, the ancient church of Saint-Germain-des-Prés. Kitty didn't actually go into this church in my book, but I had visualized her living in one of the narrow streets nearby, which had shops and a street market, and I was delighted to find such a place really and truly existed. Going down it, I passed the open doorway of an apartment block and caught sight of a gloomy atrium and a lift with a latticed sliding door, all exactly as I had envisioned.

As I roamed around the area taking photographs of sunlit squares, I caught sight of other vignettes that one might only discover by accident, wandering aimlessly with the time to stop and notice, the sort of detail that one can slip into a fictional scene. A fashion shoot with a bride and groom, a girl sitting at the window of a café reading an old Penguin paperback. There was a flower shop on the corner of a side street with an extremely narrow pavement, and any time a passerby hurried past, their clothes would brush against petals. I liked the idea of them reaching their destination smelling of lilies or roses.

After these little research trips, I would walk back to meet my son at our hotel, often via the river. It is difficult to imagine Paris without thinking of the Seine, of the graceful arcs of its bridges, some richly adorned by figures in gold leaf, others studded with ornate lamps. Was the Pont des Arts, the narrow footbridge connecting the Louvre with the Beaux Arts area of Saint-Germain and, more specifically, the Musée d'Orsay (once a railway station), a recent addition to their number? The current version of it is, but maybe Kitty would have crossed the old one from time to time. On my way back that day I strolled over it myself, delighting in the tens of thousands of padlocks clipped to its railings and gratings, following a custom started by lovers in 2008 who would then throw the keys into the water as symbols of devotion to one another. (Shortly after I returned to England, I read that these had been removed by the authorities because the sheer weight of so much love was causing the bridge to fall apart.)

Walking along the river here, past the Louvre and up toward

the great empty space between the museum and the Hotel de Ville was when I passed into a later strand in my novel, the story of Kitty's daughter, Fay, born in 1939, who visits the city in 1961 and searches for the hidden truth about her Parisian childhood.

My theme was the tricks of memory. How could Fay, I wondered, be teased into remembering what she had forgotten: her life in Paris before she was five? What kind of things would she experience in the city at age twenty-two that would whisk her back to being that childhood self that we each carry within us? I decided that it would involve re-creating the sensations that had most made an impression on her, but I was concerned for her. Some of them were associated with traumatic experiences and deep emotion.

I must have had an idiotic expression on my face as I walked along the riverbank pondering these things, because I fell victim to a clever psychological trick. From the opposite direction, an old woman approached with a young child at her side. As they drew near, she suddenly bent down and picked something up from the pavement, then held it out to me, affecting surprise, and asked in a strange accent if it was mine. I glanced at the gold wedding ring lying in her open palm and shook my head. "Someone else must have dropped it," I said, and looked about us, but there was no one else nearby.

"You have it," she said. "No use to me—I divorced." I shook my head and suggested she take it to a police station. "No. no, you have it," she insisted and she took my hand and folded my fingers around the ring. It was as I made to walk away with it that she demanded money and, too late, I realized the whole thing was a scam. The ring, when I examined it, was cheap metal and the banknote I thrust at her was chiefly to cover my embarrassment at being duped. Still, maybe she bought her hungry-looking granddaughter a sandwich with it. I comforted myself with the thought.

I'd never have fallen for something like that in London. It could only have happened in Paris, where I'd been caught up in a dream and where a lost ring fit the atmosphere of romance. I tried to work the episode into Fay's story, but it wouldn't go. Happily, little is wasted with a writer. We are magpies collecting shiny experiences, and this one became the basis of a short story set in modern Paris.

The following day, my search for specific impressions from a Paris wartime childhood that might nudge at the adult Fay's consciousness continued. Passing the plateglass windows of the tempting glamorous shops in the Champs-Élysées reminded me of the time in 1940 when they were smashed by youths because of their Jewish owners. If baby Fay had witnessed this, then the crash of a breaking bottle there twenty years later would have traumatized her adult self. A bell I heard tolling in Notre-Dame was exactly right to trigger memories of a more sinister tocsin from when she was one and escaping the Nazis with her mother. Other experiences caught me unawares: a girl at a Métro station singing an old popular song, the feel of an unusually shaped door handle, a particular fragrance of polished wood. I borrowed such things to help reconnect Fay with her infant self.

On a happier note, Fay experienced Paris in 1961 with delight-ful freshness—the scent of violets, a glimpse of models elegant in *haute couture*. I wrote how she played the violin passionately in the concerts she'd come to perform. And of course, she had to fall in love—with a man who showed her Paris's dark side. For in 1961, once again Paris was an arena for violence. France's African colony, Algeria, was struggling for independence, and the city was filled with refugees fleeing the war there. They were treated abom-inably by right-wing factions and by the French police. I wove something of these events into Fay's story to show how *ne plus ça change*—nothing changes.

This second visit over, my son and I left Paris reluctantly, he with a pile of books from the English-language bookshop Shake-speare and Company, I with a sheaf of notes and hundreds of photographs I'd taken of the city, my mind darting with ideas to thread into my novel. Paris has always been a city of stories, my novel about it one of many, yet I am convinced that during my wanderings I was gifted with a glimpse of her dark past that is entirely special and unique.

⚜ ⚜ ⚜

**Rachel Hore** was a commissioning editor in a major Lon-don publishing house before she went over to the dark side and became a writer. She is the *Sunday Times* bestselling author of eight novels, including *A Place of Secrets* and *A Week in Paris*. She lives in Norwich, Norfolk, England, and teaches creative writing at the University of East Anglia.

**Say bonjour:**
rachelhore.co.uk
Facebook: /RachelHoreAuthor
Twitter: @RachelHore

**The Paris Book:**
*A Week in Paris*

**Favorite Paris moment:**
Visiting the Musée d'Orsay for the first time. It's a marvelously converted old railway station full of light and color to show off all the modern art it contains.

**Least favorite Paris moment:**
Ordering soup "*au pot de chambre*" in a restaurant, thinking it was a joke, and it actually being served in a chamber pot.

**Favorite quote about Paris:**
"I have often dreamed of writing a book about Paris that would be like one of those long, aimless strolls on which you find none of the things you are looking for but many that you were not looking for." —Julian Green, *Paris*

**Favorite non-Paris travel destination:**
Cornwall, UK.

**Strangest must-have travel item:**
A wine-bottle stopper.

*In Paris, you can skip . . .*

Any big attraction you haven't booked in advance.
The lines for the Eiffel Tower and the George
Pompidou Center are endless.

*In Paris, you must . . .*

Visit the Père Lachaise cemetery and spot the graves
of the famous.

# SECRET EATINGS

*Julie Powell*

There must be someone, though, who knows what I mean. Probably everyone does, because of his own secret eatings.

—M. F. K. Fisher, *Serve It Forth*

I wanted so much to love Paris.

I wanted to love Paris the way an eleven-year-old girl might want to become a nun because she's watched *The Sound of Music* too many times and can't know that her fantasies of spinning deliriously in a meadow in a novice's habit are just the first simmerings of the boil of puberty. Instead of Julie Andrews, I wanted to be Jean Seberg in *Breathless*, wearing a Breton stripe shirt and pegged pants, cigarette dangling from a pouty lip. Or perhaps M. F. K. Fisher, drying sections of tangerine on top of a radiator while watching the soldiers march by on the cold cobbled street below. I was twenty-six rather than eleven the first time I flew to Paris, but the longing for ravishment was the same.

To get there, I took no vows of celibacy, but I did leave my husband at home while I went to serve as a babysitter for two preadolescent boys, which amounts to the same thing. I sat in a middle seat on the red-eye flight between a nine-year-old whining with exhaustion and an eleven-year-old whose fantasies were less about spinning in meadows and more about shoving stinking socks into his nanny's face, while their parents sat safely removed across the aisle.

We landed into a gray, drizzling morning and took a cab from the airport to an apartment at the grubby edge of the 3rd arrondissement that my employers had sublet for the trip. After climbing three flights of a dark and dingy stairwell, we knocked on a door and were let in by an icily French blonde, who showed us around a bright and coolly beautiful space, all white, tall ceilings and concrete floors, enormous succulents and art books everywhere. We were shown our rooms; mine was a space just off the living room, barely large enough to accommodate the tiny daybed pushed up against the one window. The crisp white sheets, and the view out that window, called out to me, but there was no time for lounging, for straight back out onto the street we went to find some lunch.

We chose a bistro based on two factors: how quickly we could get out of the rain, and whether two increasingly grumpy boys raised on frozen corn and chicken tenders could find something to eat there. The place where we wound up, on a bustling unbeautiful street, was brightly lit and claustrophobic, crowded with tourists in Bermuda shorts and many kids, who I suspected were just as picky as the two we had in tow. In fact, I suspected that was the reason for the crowd. We were seated in some woven plastic chairs by a terse maître d', who also handed us our comically over-size menus.

The mother had a salad, the father *steak frites*. The kids, after some dismayed flipping through the menu pages, discovered the crêpes. I, in a move that I only later recognized as a tiny (nay, invisible) act of ill-tempered rebellion, ordered the Frenchiest, most challenging thing I could find: the *foie de boeuf.*

Now, I wasn't a complete stranger to liver, beef or otherwise. I liked thin slices, fried or sautéed, medium-rare. I considered it sophisticated.

This wasn't that.

The one-pound slab of slippery brick-red organ, pooled blood spilling from the plate to the white tablecloth, made my eyes involuntarily go wide in alarm for a moment. But I was in Paris, I was brave, and I'd kind of put my rep on the line here, so I ate nearly half of the iron-tasting thing. I guessed it had been placed under a warming rack for a bit rather than actually cooked. It tasted of chewy, lukewarm blood and made me queasy. But at least I'd kept my pride intact.

We walked straight back to the apartment after our meal. The rain had stopped, but all was grumpy and gray. I stepped in dog shit; the eleven-year-old laughed at me.

⚜

For the mother and father, this was to be a social whirlwind of a trip. Dinners and galas, long days and late nights with old friends and famous artists, the whole high-end Parisian fantasy.

I watched MTV Europe. Thanks to the eleven-year-old, who

had a mulish streak, there was lots and lots of MTV Europe. I was responsible for the kids all day and most nights. I couldn't even sit on the little daybed in my little room; the smaller boy, particularly, was needy and wanted me by his side at all times to read him a story or play a game or get him a snack. I could about manage the time it took to go to the bathroom, so far as private time went. The Euro-pop music coming from the television was so aggressively awful, the Day-Glo antics on the screen so violently peppy, that relaxation was impossible anyway.

But I wanted to love Paris, I really did. So I tried.

"Hey, guys, you want to take a walk?" This was not dignified with a response.

"What about a museum?" The eleven-year-old snorted without glancing from the TV screen.

"Crêpes? I saw a stand down the street."

The nine-year-old started putting his shoes on. The eleven-year-old shrugged and switched off the remote. "I guess that'd be okay. Can we go look for a basketball court after?"

Crêpes were my salvation, my first trip to Paris.

⚜

Before that trip, the only time I'd traveled abroad was when my husband and I went to Italy for our honeymoon. Every village we stayed in, we picked one café, and got our cappuccinos there every morning, in leisurely fashion at a table on a plaza somewhere, watching the world go by. Then, before we got into our rental car for our day of sightseeing, we'd find a *salumeria*, the funkier the aroma wafting out from it, the better, and buy some sort of meat for our lunch. A hunk of cheese, a loaf of bread, a bottle of cheap red. When we got hot and hungry and tired around midday, we'd find the nearest park or picnic area or forest, eat our food and drink our wine (out of little souvenir mugs we bought outside the Vatican), and fall asleep for an hour or so before meandering on to whatever was the next dot on the map. We drove across half the country that way, taking in, together, as if with one pair of newly married eyeballs, the cobblestoned mountain villages, dark-scented churches, ruins of ancient cities. Good, simple food was our ballast.

But in Paris, it was like some optic nerve had malfunctioned. Traveling with my employers and my charges made me feel dreadfully lonely. Almost never getting to actually be alone made it worse. Even the handful of hours I did get to myself, taking in Notre-Dame, walking the Seine, visiting the Tuileries or the Eiffel Tower, it was no good. My eyes took in the sights, but there was some sort of filter, or maybe triangulation, missing. Without my husband, it didn't translate into meaning. My brain might recognize something as "beautiful" or "romantic," but my heart couldn't feel it. I wasn't falling in love with Paris, for all its chilly beauty. I could see why I should, why everyone did, but I . . . didn't.

Since then I have traveled, both with my husband and alone, to cities around the world, and I've gradually learned that overcoming this sort of lonesome blindness is really just a matter of practice. The nerve is pinched, but not destroyed, by solitude. If you keep looking hard enough, for long enough, without any particular expectation to be ravished, you can come to see a place, and maybe even know it a little, on only your and the city's terms.

But it can be work, still. Luckily for me, it turns out that while I can be too lonely to see a place from time to time, I'm very rarely too lonely to taste it. I've eaten alone, in restaurants elegant and dumpy, in the kitchens of strangers, in tiny hotel rooms and rented apartments, and while I'm sometimes too dejected or nervous to really take in the view, or the people, or the beautiful or divey bar I'm in, eventually something I put in my mouth will make me look up.

Perhaps ten years after Paris, I spent five weeks in Buenos Aires. It was the first foreign city I had been in entirely on my own, and I was paralyzed.

The first few days, I'd force myself to walk a few blocks, take in a neighborhood, then scurry back exhausted to my rented apartment. *It's a beautiful apartment*, I'd find myself justifying. (It *was* beautiful.) *I can look out the window and watch the Catholic kids at recess, see the looming church dome. I love the high ceilings, the dark wainscoting, the Wi-Fi. I can know all about Buenos Aires right here.* I slept through several afternoons.

But on one of my forced treks, I found an unassuming café on Avenida Corrientes. Gentle light, gentle people. I ordered my coffee and *churros con dulce de leche*—oh, those churros— and I watched the city waking up. Once I found the place, I returned every morning. And after I'd had my breakfast, the same breakfast every morning, I would start walking, all over the city, from the narrow cobbled streets of San Telmo to the broad tree-lined avenues of Recoleta, from the trendy shops and parks of Palermo Soho to the eye-poppingly painted facades of La Boca. I went to the horse track on my own. I got on a bus to Iguazu Falls on my own. I ate *bife de costilla* on my own, one of the only people in a restaurant at the early hour of nine thirty P.M., and the only woman sitting alone. And I was happy. It wasn't the waiter hovering and worrying over me that made me feel safe. It was the churros.

It's happened that way for me over and over. The narrow gray streets of Melbourne can be disorienting, but I discovered a bar in an alley, no larger than a walk-in closet, and a mustachioed bartender who mixed me deliriously strange cocktails, created on the spot based on what he divined my mood to be. My mental map of the city thereafter centered on that delightful pocket of peace. In Hawaii, it was ahi tuna *poke* and macaroni salad that sustained me through days of solo hikes and beach walks. In Hokkaido, I popped milk candies while checking my e-mail every morning at the local Internet café, wearing paper slippers.

But when I was in Paris, I hadn't yet learned this trick. I hadn't figured out that I could eat my way into both comfort and adventure. On my very last night, though, I got an inkling.

⚜

We never did find a basketball court, though the boys and I walked the city every day, for as long I could bribe them. I looked up parks in my guidebook, figuring those would be good bets, but they wound up being ornate, beautiful, meticulously designed places where the police rousted you if you sat on the grass, and sports had no toehold. The eleven-year-old hated them. In the hours we wandered, he'd go from bored to petulant to, by the end of the afternoon, sincerely disturbed. For this b-ball-obsessed New York City kid, there was something deeply alien about a city without a pickup game going on somewhere within five blocks at any given moment. It was no wonder, really, that he sighed and scuffed his shoes and wanted his MTV. He wasn't afraid, exactly, but it was something close; he was unmoored. "Can I have another crêpe?"

On our last day, we returned to the apartment by a different path, and when we were just a couple of blocks away, came across a bakery. We'd walked by many bakeries, of course, but the aroma wafting out from this particular one, for some reason, stopped me in my tracks.

"What are you doing?"

"Hold on one second, I've got to grab something."

The inside of the bakery smelled even better than the outside, and was cozy warm. A gleaming glass case was neatly filled with beautiful pastries, but what caught my eye, the scent that had drawn me in, was the stack of baguettes in a basket behind the counter. "Do you want a *pain au chocolat*?"

"You said crêpes!"

"Okay, okay . . ."

The extent of my French is more or less *s'il vous plaît, merci*, and a bunch of words for various foodstuffs. But with enough

nodding and smiling and pointing, I was able to procure the baguette I suddenly wanted desperately. On our outing, I had seen
several spiffy-looking Parisians carrying around baguettes; maybe
having one would bring me one step closer to Seberg territory.

And then we went to the crêpe stand. *Deux Nutella crêpes,
s'il vous plaît.*

❦

It was the last night before we were to return to the States, and
the kids' parents had one last big night out. Amid the bustle of
mislaid jewelry and packing bags for the early flight the next day,
of persuading kids to wash their hands before the crêpe-free dinner
I forced upon them ("Don't worry that the package is in French, it's
just peas"), the fact of the baguette slipped my mind entirely until
several hours later. After the usual compulsory MTV watching,
some pleading for stories, and complaining about bedtimes, the
kids finally went to sleep. Shutting the bedroom door was a wonderful relief.

I padded across the cold concrete floor to the kitchen. The
apartment was lit only by the ambient glow of a large city at
night, and a single pendant lamp over the kitchen island. In the
pool of warm light was a bottle of wine, and the baguette. My
stomach rumbled. I got out the butter, popped the cork, and tore
off a piece of bread, munching as I crossed the apartment to my
tiny room.

I laid the entire package of butter, the baguette, the wine bottle, and a glass out on the windowsill. Then I curled up onto the
cozy, small, wrought-iron daybed in the dark and stared out the

window at a nighttime romantic vista I had never noticed before: a sea of pitched roofs, the building's grimy cobbled courtyard below, an orange pinprick down there where the old woman who supervised the building sat, enjoying one last cigarette. I drank red wine and ate a baguette like I had never had before. Crisp, caramel-brown crust snapping between my teeth. Airy, tender, ever so slightly yeasty middle, slathered with good French butter. I ate the entire thing, drank the entire bottle of wine.

It was the first time I allowed myself to see Paris, to be *in* it a little.

Gazing across rooftops in the dark, I got to thinking about my older charge. Despite the sulking and the bad pop music, I was fond of the kid. Back in New York, he was still sullen, a teenager in all but years, but he was also witty and mischievous, with a gleam in his eye. Here in Paris, he was glum, and staunchly resisted the very idea of fun. His eyes were constantly trained on his Game Boy or the TV or, if he was forced outside, at his sneakers. But standing by that crêpe stand that afternoon, Nutella smeared on his chin, I saw the kid I knew from back home. A grin, a glint. He even made fun of me. He was comfortable, for a moment, in a place he found profoundly uncomfortable. I crunched down on a hunk of that glorious bread that night, licked the creamiest butter I'd ever had from my fingers.

I drifted off amid the crumbs in my sheets.

⚜

That was twenty years ago, give or take. Those two boys are grown men out there in the world somewhere. Traveling, perhaps, with their girlfriends or husbands or children (or babysitters), or all by themselves.

I've never had children, which was less a decision and more a combination of dilly-dallying and bum genetics, and is a story for another day. But I like to think I did a little parenting during the time I spent with those boys. That I might have shown them some new flavor, some great book, some sense of adventure. And I'd like to meet them again, once, just to see what sort of men they've grown into. I'd like to ask them about Paris. What do they remember?

In her book *Serve It Forth,* M. F. K. Fisher speaks of what she calls "secret eatings," private food rituals. She writes of drying tangerine sections on a radiator; I recall that on the rare occasions when I eat a bag of M&M's, I must eat two of the same color at a time. Fisher thinks of these secrets as attached to place and time; the tangerine story takes place in Strasbourg, though in my imagination, when I read it, it's always Paris, between the wars. She had the revelation, as I eventually did, that food and drink are to a person alone both balm and alarm clock; something to soothe and something to open your eyes. It's the kind of quotidian realization you come to, slowly or all at once, that can change you, in small and profound ways.

I may never come to love Paris the way so many do; neither may those two boys who are now men. But I think I'd be satisfied if I only knew they remember the Nutella crêpes. And if they then told me about the *elote* vendor they visit every time they're in Mexico City. Or the *tom yam kung* eaten beachside every time they visit Thailand. Then I'd know that something really had begun in Paris. For them, and for me.

❦ ❦ ❦

**Julie Powell** is the author of the critically acclaimed *New York Times* bestselling memoir *Julie & Julia: My Year of Cooking Dangerously*, which was adapted into a major motion picture starring Meryl Streep and Amy Adams. Her second book, *Cleaving: A Story of Marriage, Meat, and Obsession*, was published by Little, Brown and Company.

*Say bonjour:*
   Twitter: @licjulie

*The Paris Book:*
   *Julie & Julia: My Year of Cooking Dangerously*

*Favorite Paris moment:*
   Being asked by André Cointreau, over lunch at a lavishly elegant private club, how I experienced my fame, existentially speaking. Also, I bought the coolest eyeglasses I've ever owned—years later I still mourn my mother's dog chewing them up.

*Least favorite Paris moment:*
   Shopping in a boutique for a small friend of mine, and having the salesgirl rip a top I was looking at out of my hands as if I was going to try to squeeze into the thing right then and there.

*Favorite quote about Paris:*
   "Cities have sexes: London is a man, Paris a woman, and New York a well-adjusted transsexual."—Angela Carter

**Favorite book about Paris:**

I'd be a traitor if I didn't list *My Life in France* by Julia Child. But *Suite Française* by Irène Némirovsky is wonderful, too, and I'm a sucker for good spy novels and love Alan Furst—many of his books are set in full or in part in Paris.

**Favorite non-Paris travel destination:**

Too many to count—Rome, Tanzania, Buenos Aires, Los Angeles . . . but I will always go back to Villanueva, New Mexico.

**Strangest must-have travel item:**

I don't think it's strange that I always have a corkscrew.

⚜ ⚜ ⚜

# UNTIL WE MEET AGAIN

*Lauren Willig*

There's nothing like almost getting arrested to start a trip off right.

I hadn't arrived in Paris intending to make trouble. It was meant to be an easy trip. Paris was *terra cognita* for me, or so I thought. I'd been visiting and revisiting the city since my first trip with my grandfather nearly twenty years earlier. I had always viewed Paris as particularly mine. This was because I knew, in the flat, bright way in which children know things, that my mother had once been a little Parisian girl, that she had been born within view of Notre-Dame and gone to school at an *école maternelle* run by long-skirted nuns like Miss Clavel in the Madeline books.

There were pictures in an album of my mother with her hair flipped up at the ends, looking impossibly foreign and French, or, earlier still, chasing pigeons in a sepia-toned garden that might have been the Jardin du Luxembourg or the Jardin des Tuileries or some entirely different Parisian park that still managed to look entirely the same.

That this was her history, not mine, didn't occur to me. I only knew that when I announced my Parisian bona fides in middle school French classes with a faux modest *"Ma mère est née à Paris,"* my grade miraculously went up, even if my accent was far more Upper East Side than Rive Droite.

So when I set out from my hotel that jet-lagged morning, with my notebook under my arm, I was really quite sure I knew just where I was going. It was Paris. I'd been there enough times that I'd lost count: with family, with fellow students, with work colleagues, and with a long-ago boyfriend with whom I'd nearly broken up on the Pont des Arts.

Possibly, it would have been wiser to have napped first. Possibly, it would have been wiser to have eaten something more substantial than a Nature Valley bar that had been living on the bottom of my bag since . . . well, probably since somewhere around my third book. Possibly, everything would have happened as it happened anyway. Just ask Sartre.

On this particular trip, I was researching my eighth novel, *The Orchid Affair*, which was not, for the record, about horticultural indiscretions, but spies during the Napoleonic Wars, who, both fictionally and, bizarrely enough, in real life, appeared to have a penchant for botanical monikers. My fictional spy was named the Silver Orchid, sent undercover into the household of a high-ranking member of Napoleon's Ministry of Police disguised as a humble governess. And if this sounds a bit like *The Sound of Music* without nuns or Nazis, plus a few people in black masks creeping over windowsills, well, yes, that was the general idea. Just substitute baguettes for strudel. I intended to research those baguettes quite diligently, preferably with butter, and maybe a bit of jam.

But first I needed to learn a bit about the Paris police department, the Préfecture of Police: its workings, its personnel, its physical landscape. My book was to open with the hero, that high-ranking police official, interrogating someone at the offices of the Préfecture. Which is where I hit one of those many frustrations that comes with writing fiction set in early nineteenth-century Paris: They'd torn it down. They'd also torn down the Abbey Prison, another significant location in the novel. The place where L'Abbaye had stood was, according to my best calculation, somewhere in the middle of the boulevard Saint-Germain, a fact I discovered while almost being mowed down by a moped. When it comes to giving historical novelists headaches, Paris's mid-nineteenth-century architect Baron Haussmann has a great deal to answer for.

Mercifully, there was—oh, joy! Oh, rapture unforeseen!—a Museum of the Préfecture of Police, which, if the website was to be believed, contained a small treasure of information about French police work past and present. The museum was located at 4 rue de la Montagne-Sainte-Geneviève. The website showed pictures of rooms tidily lined with glass cases, framed documents on the walls, mannequins wearing uniforms from the 1870s with their hair styled in unfortunate *coiffeurs* from the 1970s. As I set off down the slope—they weren't joking about that mountain in the street name—I could picture the building I was looking for, a narrow townhouse museum with the exhibits arranged along four or five floors, connected by a steep stair.

Those of you familiar with Paris will have already spotted

my error. They don't do townhouse museums. Or at least not townhouse museums like that. Paris doesn't have townhouses, it has *hotels*, another beast entirely. The Musée de Cluny, the Musée Jacquemart-André, the Musée Cognacq-Jay all sprawl out along the sides of a courtyard, long and low. Intellectually, I knew that. But I was a native New Yorker who had spent some time living in England; the house in my head was narrow and redbrick, with a slate roof and dormer windows.

Needless to say, there was no narrow redbrick townhouse at 4 rue de la Montagne-Sainte-Geneviève. Instead, as I approached the bottom of the hill, the ground cleared. Dozens of police cars clustered around a modern building that looked like a concrete block set on stilts. Gendarmes in puffy black jackets loitered next to their cars, smoking cigarettes.

I retraced my steps up the hill, convinced that I must have missed the museum. Up and down, down and up, first one side of the street, then the other.

As I circled the police station again and yet again, the policemen began to take note, giving me the stink-eye over their half-smoked cigarettes. I couldn't tell whether that was a reaction to my casing the joint or my research wardrobe: stacked-heel loafers, jeans, and a button-down shirt that was Palm Beach pink rather than Paris black, my hair sporting that "finger stuck in a light socket" chic that comes with sleeping fitfully in an upright seat on an overnight flight. Definitely not *comme il faut*.

Did you have an iPhone in 2009? I didn't. And my cell phone hadn't been configured for international use. I stood there, on the rue de la Montagne-Sainte-Geneviève, just out of sight of those suspicious gendarmes, trying to decide what to do. The logical thing would have been to move on to the next item on my list, the Musée Cognacq-Jay, where there was an exhibit on Marguerite Gérard, a female French artist of the Revolution. (Just try to say that three times fast.) But that was way on the other side of the river, along with the other stops on my list for tomorrow. And I'd made a *plan*.

Everything seems vaguely apocalyptic when you're overtired. In my jet-lagged brain, I decided that if the museum wasn't there, then the whole trip was wasted; if the whole trip was wasted, I was never going to be able to write the book; if I never wrote the book, I would have to cancel the contract and return the advance; and then—oh, horrors!—I was going to have to go back to being a lawyer.

I had to find that museum.

I stopped a few passersby with that nervous tourist smile and a polite request for directions, and got the usual assortment of people too busy to bother, good Samaritans who directed me to contradictory locations, most at least a few Métro stops away, and someone hawking her brother's restaurant.

I vaguely remembered that *Sesame Street* had instructed, when lost, to find a policeman. Well, I was lost and there were certainly a lot of policemen about.

I made my way up to the nearest squad car.

*"Où se trouve le Musée de la Préfecture de Police?"* I asked, for the five hundredth time. I was tempted to ask for the pen of the cousin of my aunt, in proper middle school French textbook

fashion, but then they might feel obligated to write out a report about it.

The police officer looked at me like I was an idiot. Or an American, the two being largely synonymous. "Here."

I looked around. I still didn't see a museum, unless one was hiding under the police car. "Where?"

The policeman rolled his eyes, said something to his partner, and escorted me, with exaggerated dignity, to the glass doors that led into the forbidding concrete block.

"Here," he repeated, but a little more loudly and slowly this time.

And then he went back to smoking his Gauloise.

The lobby was full of people doing official-seeming things, families waiting on chairs, policemen and harried-looking bureaucrats in suits hurrying to and fro. There was someone who appeared to be in the middle of being arraigned right behind me. I waited my turn at the reception desk and asked, with my best I'm-just-a-stupid-American-please-don't-be mad-at-me eyelash flutter, "*Où se trouve le Musée de la Préfecture de Police?*"

The man jerked his finger toward a large sign on the wall. "Third floor."

I looked where he had pointed, and sure enough, there it was. The building directory. Official police business this, official police business that . . . museum.

Who puts a museum in an active police station?

I decided not to share that thought. I thanked the man and got out of the way of the brawl that was starting to develop in the lobby behind me. There was, I presume, an elevator. But there were a number of people clumped around it and a door to a stairwell just ahead. New Yorkers pride ourselves on taking the more strenuous way. Two flights of stairs? No problem.

On such small decisions do our lives hinge.

The stairs were surprisingly broad, institutional, and quiet. I counted my way up the flights to the third floor. There was no signage, just a door, but the man had said three—the sign he had pointed to, for that matter, had also said three—and the door opened when I pushed it, so in I went.

And that was when the shouting started.

In my jet-lagged fog, I had forgotten that the French count floors as the Brits do: the ground floor, *then* the first floor, which Americans would count as the second. I was one floor off.

Oops.

I'm still not sure what was on that floor, but whatever it was, I wasn't supposed to be there. And I mean I *really* wasn't supposed to be there.

I tend to make those sorts of mistakes a lot in Paris, more so than when traveling other places, where I'm very aware of being foreign and very careful to mind my P's and Q's, consulting my guidebook, following the instructions, speaking in English and hoping other people do the same. In Paris, it isn't the big things that trip me up; I can find my way to the bathroom and navigate the Métro. It's the little things: the numbering of floors, the wrong pronoun. When I'm away from Paris, it feels familiar and beloved, rather like Franglais; when I'm there, I tend to be rapidly disabused of the notion that I can navigate the city or speak the language.

My first memory of Paris is, as a small person, asking for "*de la lait*"—some milk.

"*Du*," replied the waiter dourly.

"Pardon?"

"*Du lait*," he corrected, and addressed me in English thereafter.

It's easy to think one knows Paris. Paris is the property of the world, everyone's romantic weekend getaway. As with New York, we're blasted with images of it all the time: the Eiffel Tower with "Paris is for lovers!" scrawled across it, or a glossy picture of the Arc de Triomphe or les Pyramides. And, as with New York, the bits we're shown are always far from the life of the city, which isn't one city at all, but a hundred, or a thousand, some overlapping, some at odds, all going on at once, everyone's reality a little bit different: the American expat working at a law firm on the Place Vendôme, the medievalist researching at the Bibliothèque Nationale, the novelist haplessly attempting to find the Museum of the Préfecture of Police.

Recently, I researched a book that didn't happen, a saga set in Paris during the 1890s, World War I, and World War II, about an American heiress who marries a French nobleman, thinking, because her grandmother was French, that she can learn the city and charm the upper crust, that she can be more French than American. Like me, she was certain the Parisian *je ne sais quoi* was more inherited than learned.

The book began in 1889 with the Exposition Universelle and the opening of the Eiffel Tower and ended in 1940 with the Germans marching down the Champs-Élysées. Suddenly, so much about Paris that had seemed like a nuisance—basically anything that had happened after 1815—took on new meaning and resonance. The boulevard Saint-Germain wasn't just Baron Haussmann's vicious plan to foil writers of Napoleonic fiction (and annoy those people who like to put up barricades and sing about hearing people singing)—it was where my heroine's snobby sister-in-law would have lived; where she might meet Monsieur de Montesquieu and his sycophant, that scribbler Proust, at a reception.

In the end, after months of work, I gave up on the book. The reason? It wasn't about the characters anymore. They were mere paper cutouts against the much more vivid backdrop of Paris itself: French politics, French culture, the experience of being an American in Paris. So I put my Paris book aside and went back to writing a story that actually had some story in it, but with a renewed appreciation of the layered nature of Paris, a city that exists in different times for different people, some searching for the Revolution, the fall of the Bastille, the tumbrils, others for the dance halls of the Belle Époque, all Art Nouveau posters and Champagne from a high-heeled shoe.

But it's impossible to sift the one entirely from the other. The layers are too closely bound together. Are you a Victor Hugo fan? You can see his apartments, a nineteenth-century domicile in a seventeenth-century arcade. A medievalist? Once you come in through those modern glass pyramids, an excavation at the bottom of the Louvre shows you bits of the medieval castle. When I went looking for the lost Dauphin at the Conciergerie, there was a fashion show in progress in the main hall, models strutting down the flagstones, white faux frost trees disguising the ancient stone walls, techno music invading the cell where an effigy of Marie Antoinette says her final prayers.

Paris resists being easily known. It is a city within a city within a city, layers of history, sometimes overlapping, sometimes at odds, folding together in a way that can be disorienting to those of us from younger civilizations, allowing us to trip over one thing when we are expecting another: galleries of avant-garde art housed in sixteenth-century buildings, trendy fashion shows in an ancient prison—and a history museum in a modern police station.

The police were really very nice about my gaffe. Either they decided I was suitably harmless, or, more likely, it had something to do with the way their eyes glazed as I attempted to explain the plot of the book I was researching in my extremely stilted and ungrammatical schoolgirl French. They even escorted me to the museum proper, although it's hard to say whether that was politeness or policy.

As for the museum itself, it was everything I had wanted it to be, other than not being in a townhouse. There was a painting of the Old Préfecture, rickety and atmospheric, and ledgers in glass cases, containing accounts of interrogations and trials in faded but still legible writing. Along one wall was an exhibit about the seventeenth-century Affair of the Poisons, a scandal in which several high-ranking courtiers were implicated in a dastardly plot involving black magic and, yes, poison.

Mannequins in Napoleonic uniform posed in front of period maps and cases containing papers and passes. Here, I was on solid ground. Seventeenth-century Paris? No problem. I had spent my grad school years reading seventeenth-century correspondence: The misspellings and archaic French come more easily to me than the front page of *Le Monde*. All the historical figures mentioned on the walls were old friends or at least old acquaintances. Paris was home again—at least, until anybody actually spoke to me or I tried to take the stairs somewhere.

The Paris that feels so familiar to me when I'm away, the French that I speak so fluently in my dreams, the pictures of my mother in a Parisian park: They're all a form of never-never-land, a Paris that was, or might have been, but most decidedly isn't now. And if it ever was, it will most likely have changed five minutes from now. Cities tend to do that.

I wish I could say I learned my lesson that day in the police station, but there's a part of me that will always fall for the trap of feeling at home in Paris—until we meet again.

⚜ ⚜ ⚜

**Lauren Willig** is the *New York Times* and *USA Today* bestselling author of the Pink Carnation series, as well as several stand-alone works of historical fiction, including *The Other Daughter*. After graduating from Yale, she went on to collect a graduate degree in history from Harvard and a JD from Harvard Law. She lives in New York, where she now writes full-time.

### Say bonjour:

laurenwillig.com

Facebook: /LaurenWillig

Twitter: @LaurenWillig

### The Paris Books:

*The Secret History of the Pink Carnation*

*The Orchid Affair*

*The Garden Intrigue*

*The English Wife* (coming 2018)

### Favorite Paris moment:

That moment when you sink, still slightly jet-lagged, into the wrought-iron chair in the *boulangerie* across from your hotel with a *café crème* and a *pain aux amandes*. Nothing tastes as good as that first mouthful of coffee and flaky pastry.

### Least favorite Paris moment:

Those little shuttle buses between terminals at Charles de Gaulle. I'm always convinced I'm going to get on the wrong one and wind up in Normandy.

### Favorite quote about Paris:

"Paris is worth a mass."—Henri IV, master of understatement and wearer of exceptionally perky ruffs. My version: "Paris is worth six hours in coach."

**Favorite book about Paris:**

Nancy Mitford's *Don't Tell Alfred* is one of my favorite Paris-set novels, a hilarious send-up of not only the French, but the absurdities of Brits and Americans in Paris, as well, with all the cross-cultural misunderstanding that ensues. It's a comedy, but it's also a love song to Paris in all of its full-skirted postwar chic.

**Favorite non-Paris travel destination:**

Scotland. Edinburgh is one of the friendliest cities in the world. And I may be one of three people ever who actually likes haggis.

**In Paris, you must . . .**

Last-minute, standing-room-only tickets to the *Comedie Française*. There's nothing to make you feel like you're getting the real Paris experience like catching a bit of Molière, *deus ex machina* and all, seen imperfectly around someone's very large head.

⚜ ⚜ ⚜

# A GOOD IDEA?

*Therese Anne Fowler*

I don't remember a time when I didn't yearn to go to Paris. When I was a teen, my urge was to run away to Paris to escape a depressing small town where nothing inspired me and my every move was criticized and constricted by my overbearing, abusive stepfather. To be honest, I would have run away to almost anywhere if I'd believed I could survive on my own—but Paris, star of so many of the films I'd seen and the books I'd read, was the dream destination. It was, Julia Ormond in *Sabrina* promised, "always a good idea."

In Paris, not only would I be free of my stepfather, I would be taller, prettier, more confident—and of course I would be greyhound-thin. I'd have luxurious, long dark hair (though I am blond), and speak French like a native. I'd learn to drink *café au lait* (*avec sucre—beaucoup*, because I hated coffee) and eat escargots and croissants and other French-word foods. I would read Rabelais (whoever he was; I'd heard the name in *Music Man*). I would buy Gauloises and pretend to smoke them, for looks. In my shabby but elegant garret, to which surely I would one day

bring a tall, dark lover To-Be-Named, I would pen heartfelt po-
ems filled with ennui, and croon along with Edith Piaf records.
I would feed pigeons at my windowsills. I'd leave milk in a sau-
cer for the fat, contented cat that would sleep on my building's
stoop. I would lose myself in Paris, and in doing so, find myself.
Wasn't that how it was done?

But lacking a passport, money, and nerve, I did not run away
to my dream city, or anywhere. Instead, I escaped into books,
until I was old enough to finish high school and leave home in a
more ordinary way. *Quel dommage*—especially given that soon
after, I got married and went to the Republic of the Philippines
for three years as a too-young Air Force wife. My life at Clark
Air Base bore zero resemblance to my Parisian ideal (and little
resemblance to my marriage ideal, for that matter). I'd gone away
as a teenage newlywed and returned as a demoralized "dependent wife," largely because my own goals and interests had been
constricted all that time. I hadn't consciously chosen marriage as
an escape, but it would function as one naturally, right? Wrong.
When I returned to the United States at age twenty-two, I was,
in ways that would take decades to fully understand, more lost
than before.

❧

Paris was still my dream destination twenty-five years later, after
I'd become a novelist who'd spent a lot of time in Paris on the
page, but none, so far, in life. My fictional adventure had been
with Zelda Fitzgerald, famed "crazy" wife of America's Sweetheart
author F. Scott Fitzgerald—a spirited woman whose youthful

desire for escape and adventure, in the early 1900s, was not so different from my own. But at forty-seven, my hopes and expectations for the city and myself had changed dramatically from what they'd once been. That disaffected teen, that too-young bride, was now a divorced mother of two grown-up sons. I possessed two college degrees and wrote fiction, not poetry. My ennui was gone. I'd become quite fond of *café au lait* (and with only *un peu de sucre* now). I was not appreciably taller, prettier, or thinner, and my hair was still blond, but I had found my tall, dark lover—and he was taking me to France.

As a focus of the trip, I hoped to uncover the Paris that had, just as World War I was ending, enticed the Lost Generation with its siren song. I yearned to see for myself why Zelda and Scott Fitzgerald, whom I'd come to know intimately through my research and portrayal of their lives, hadn't been most keenly drawn to, say, Rome, or Prague, or Geneva, or London, or Madrid, or . . . ? I wanted to hear that siren song through the 1920s ears I'd developed while writing about those lost souls, let the tune and the rhythms tell me why Paris was "always a good idea."

An overnight flight from Charlotte, North Carolina, had my man and me watching the sunrise while cruising, first over Ireland, then over a blanket of clouds that obscured most of England and all of France as the jet slowly descended toward Charles de Gaulle Airport in the outskirts of Paris, nary a glimpse of the Eiffel Tower to be had. Deplaning into a terminal that looked like a relic from the *Jetsons* era, I was tired but excited. I'd finally made it to Paris! Sort of! First we would rent a car and drive south, way south, six hours south on the A71/77 to a little town called Cahors and the summer home of dear friends who couldn't wait to induct me into French countryside life.

In our little Euro-car, we set off into the drizzly morning's rush-hour traffic, jet-lagged and language-challenged, our first order of business being to persuade the GPS guide to speak to us in English, *s'il vous plaît*. There are only so many tests a sleep-deprived middle-aged brain wants at two A.M. Eastern Time when there's lots of highway ahead and no sleep in sight.

After several excellent days exploring Cahors and the Lot Valley, we went farther south still, to trail after the Fitzgeralds on the French Riviera. As Zelda had done during her first months in France, I hiked the stony Mediterranean cliffs at Cap d'Antibes and admired Gerald Murphy's beach and swam in the azure water while luxurious yachts anchored farther offshore. I drank a 23-euro gin cocktail called Green Remedy on the patio of the Fitzgeralds' former home (now a hotel), once known as Villa St. Louis, where Zelda had likewise watched the sun drop behind the low mountains and darkening sea. And all the while, as I trekked up the cobblestone hills in Haut de Cagnes, as I channeled Van Gogh at the center of Arles, as I traversed the old Roman aqueduct Pont du Gard, the Eiffel Tower's rotating beacon beckoned me. The Parisian sirens sang.

❧

Paris-bound, we turned in the rental car and gave ourselves over to Rail Europe for a zip through the countryside. After arriving at Gare du Nord, where I stood outside the station gazing at the sheer Paris-ness of the scene, the heart of my adventure began. Now I would get to see the flats the Fitzgeralds rented as they moved again and again, trying to find stability in what was becoming a tumultuous marriage. I'd frequent their favorite cafés and bars, find their friends' homes, meander through the parks and markets and the Bois de Boulogne, visit the Louvre and Versailles—and see it all through Zelda's increasingly disenchanted eyes. I would stroll around the Luxembourg Garden pond as they'd done with their young daughter, Scottie, while she sailed a model boat. I would walk along the Seine in the moonlight, where they might have gone for solace when the middling reviews and sales reports for *The Great Gatsby* came in. Zelda, the aspiring painter; Zelda, the dancer-in-training; Zelda, the frustrated writer; Zelda, the flapper-muse-mother-wife whose ambitions upset her authoritarian husband, whose escape from the stifling life of her traditional Southern home was not turning out as planned. What was *her* Parisian ideal, there in the hot center of the Jazz Age? In a word: fulfillment.

On any given 1920s night, when the city was occupied by familiar expats like Gertrude Stein, Pablo Picasso, Ezra Pound, Ernest Hemingway, T. S. Eliot, Sylvia Beach, John Dos Passos, and Salvador Dalí, you might find a café table occupied by a composer, a painter, a novelist, a poet, a choreographer, a photographer, a sax player, everyone drinking, smoking, laughing, and arguing. They'd migrated to Paris in the wake of the war and the influenza pandemic, which killed more than fifty million people. Disillusioned, disheartened, looking for camaraderie and inspiration in a place where they could afford to live on almost no money, they created an open society where polygamy and infidelity were simply experiments in altering the social norms. "Normal" behavior was passé.

Zelda, having partied her way through New York City and St. Paul and Westport and Great Neck and the Riviera before rooting here, was no longer the lively but naive Montgomery girl she'd been a few years earlier. She was wiser, time-tested, vivid, a woman in search of her own identity, of meaning for herself. Paris was a city with its arms flung wide to embrace her.

⚜

Like Zelda, I had once followed a husband from one state to another, from my home country to a foreign one, always in service of his career and his desires. Like Zelda, I'd never lived independently before marriage; I was younger than my husband; I believed fully in marriage and family and the commitment I'd made; I tried to mold myself to my role and his needs. Also like Zelda, I chafed against the expectations and restrictions of that role, struggled with identifying and pursuing my own interests, grew dissatisfied and depressed. Too young, too unguided, too trusting of my husband's "wisdom," I did as Zelda had done: I tried to do it all.

For her, this meant doing the Charleston on tabletops, but it also meant supervising the household staff and tending her daughter's nannies and assuaging her husband's insecurities, while painting, writing short stories, and going, daily, to ballet lessons with the aim of joining a professional company. In a competitive studio where she was the oldest in her class, she attempted to put everything else aside in pursuit of that singular goal. She might, if she worked hard enough, make her aging (in ballerina terms) body meet the demands of Diaghilev's Ballet Russes—or if not that, another national company. She might prove to her husband and to herself that a wife and mother could be an artist of any kind, all on her own, no longer in need of being known first as Mrs. F. Scott Fitzgerald.

Her teacher, the Russian expat prima ballerina Madame Liubov Egorova, kept her in the Advanced class by merit. Many of the women writers she knew encouraged her pursuit of any career she desired. Paris, in all its beauty and tradition and bohemian wildness, had embraced Zelda and was holding a place for her—but it hardly mattered because Scott wouldn't let her go. If she left him, he would use the existing laws to his advantage and keep their daughter. She couldn't leave Scottie, and she refused to give up ballet, seeking in her ever-more-obsessive effort another means of escape. In losing the battle, she eventually broke down and, for a time, lost herself.

I was luckier. I lived in a time of fairer laws and better opportunities for divorced women. When I left my marriage—*because* I left my marriage—the world opened up for me. I would have to work hard, but I had a path to a truly fulfilling version of myself, and of Paris. And although fourteen years would pass before I got there, when I did, she greeted me like a lover. I could have stayed. I might yet.

⚜

Is Paris always a good idea? From the rooftop of my hotel in the Saint-Germain district where the Fitzgeralds and many of their friends had lived, I looked out over the rooftops and the dark, slowly moving Seine, and thought of Zelda's experiences here. I thought of the immigrant taxi drivers and peddlers and gypsies I'd seen, people who'd also come with high hopes and vivid dreams who did and still do exist on the fringes, living off the tourists, worrying about their fates. Night fell, and the Eiffel Tower put on its lighted cloak. Its beacon swept across the vista—not solely as a welcome, it now seemed to me, but also as a warning: Dangerous shoals may be in your path. Beware. The sirens sing, *Come to Paris, we have it all. Music and art and history and culture and food and wine and romance.* But the light says, consider, too, what—or who—you're bringing with you. Consider what all of that weighs. Expectation can be impossibly heavy, depending. Come anyway. Come to Paris with your eyes open to both the wonders and the risks. As with love, terrible or great things may await you. Embrace it, and see.

⚜ ⚜ ⚜

**Therese Anne Fowler** is the *New York Times* bestselling author of *Z: A Novel of Zelda Fitzgerald.* She holds a BA in sociology/cultural anthropology and an MFA in creative writing. An Illinois native, she transplanted herself to North Carolina in 1995 but has yet to take a shine to collard greens.

*Say bonjour:*
    thereseannefowler.com
    Facebook: /ThereseAnneFowler.Books
    Twitter: @ThereseFowler

*The Paris Book:*
  *Z: A Novel of Zelda Fitzgerald*

*Favorite Paris moment:*
  Visiting the Luxembourg Gardens in
  summertime. Sculptures, flower gardens,
  trees, fountains, the Grand Bassin, the Palace,
  the playgrounds, the bocce courts . . . It's
  simply a restful, gorgeous, genuinely French
  place to spend some important-to-schedule
  downtime.

*Least favorite Paris moment:*
  Being accosted by a very insistent group of
  peddlers on the pathway up to Sacré-Coeur. There
  were several men crowded around me, touching
  my hands, speaking rapidly all at once, trying
  to persuade me to buy one of their crafts. I had
  to forcibly push my way out of the circle. It
  was scary.

*Favorite book about Paris:*
  *The Elegance of the Hedgehog* by Muriel Barbery—it's
  smart, engaging, tender, amusing, and thought-
  provoking.

*Song that reminds you of Paris:*
  "Free Man in Paris" by Joni Mitchell—it made me
  imagine Paris as an ideal escape. "I was a free man
  in Paris / I felt unfettered and alive."

*Favorite non-Paris travel destination:*
> There are a lot of places I have yet to see, but one
> place I've returned to numerous times is Key West,
> Florida. But you have to get beyond the initial
> Duval Street tourist nonsense to really appreciate the
> town and all it has to offer.

*Strangest must-have travel item:*
> Sudoku puzzle book. Sudoku is the only thing I've
> found that can distract me when there's bad
> turbulence during a flight.

⚜ ⚜ ⚜

# PARIS ALONE

*Maggie Shipstead*

I sat motionless at my desk, breathing shallowly, my fingers resting on my laptop's keyboard. He knocked again, waited, knocked a little louder, waited. Under the apartment door, his feet cast shadows on the dark green linoleum. I didn't make a sound. Finally, he went on his way, footsteps receding. After a minute, the hall lights, which were on a timer, clicked out, and there was only darkness under the door.

The phone had rung a few times the previous day, and I hadn't answered. I knew who was calling. It was the same man who had just knocked: not a stalker or a creep, actually, but the Swiss composer who lived across the hall, an affable, fortyish guy with a mop of dark curls. I'd met him in the elevator earlier in the week. According to Google, he composed operas—not just any operas: underwater operas. (In related news, it turns out there are underwater operas. The world is a marvelous place!)

I had no friends in Paris and no reason to turn my nose up at someone who might or might not have been part humpback whale, but friendship, at the time, wasn't something I was after.

In fact, when faced with a friendly overture, I was capable only of evasive maneuvers. I was alone, you see, which for me isn't a moment-to-moment condition, easily changed, but a way of being. Solitude is a well I fall (or jump) into from time to time and don't try to climb out of. I sit down there and enjoy the quiet.

This was the end of January 2012. I had been in Paris for almost a month, with two more to go. The Swiss composer and I were both residents at the Cité Internationale des Arts, a complex of 270 live/work studio apartments for artists in the trendy 4th arrondissement neighborhood of the Marais. Most of the apartments, or *ateliers*, were underwritten by arts organizations or universities or entire nations that also chose the residents, though a small number were managed by the Cité directly. Mine belonged to Stanford University, where I'd spent the previous two years on a writing fellowship, but the plaques on the other doors along my hallway mostly identified chilly European countries not known for garrulous people: Norway, Finland, Austria, Switzerland. Being the standout hermit in such company was, I think, something of an achievement.

Completed in 1965, the Cité's main building is a massive concrete block checkered with narrow, aluminum-framed windows. It stands at 18 rue de l'Hôtel de Ville, smack on the right bank of the Seine, bookended by the Pont Marie and the Pont Louis-Philippe. Its exterior has an aesthetic kinship with, perhaps, an automotive air filter, and it makes a startlingly Brutalist entry in Paris's grand riverside parade of elegant edifices. I lived in a smaller annex nestled on a side street between a hip artisanal coffee roaster and the city's Holocaust memorial. Beyond the memorial and its security guards and ticket window insulated by several inches of bulletproof glass was a high school, and beyond that was an extraordinary little bakery where I went to buy bread and pastries and to fail at comprehending the rapid stream of numbers spoken by the cashier. I would hand over a random assortment of bills and coins—say, €7,35 when I owed €3,76—and gaze haughtily into space while I waited for most of it to be handed back, pretending my intention all along had been to set a change-making challenge.

Inside, the Cité's annex looked like a repurposed Soviet bloc government building: polished concrete, wood veneer, long, dark, hushed hallways floored in that green linoleum. My studio's small kitchen had a hot plate, electric kettle, and mini fridge, and the spacious, sunny, high-ceilinged main room was fitted out with a twin bed, bookshelf, dresser, table, easel, and giant white-painted corkboards where, if I were a visual artist, I might pin my work. The bathroom had a shower the size of a coffin and what my brother described, when he passed through town, as a prison toilet: lidless, black-seated, flushed by leaning one's whole weight on a steel button in the wall. The day I arrived, a Cité employee came to take away the spare sheets and blanket from the rickety trundle bed stored under mine, an economy that came to seem especially stingy after I realized the central heating turned off every night from eleven until six, the coldest hours, when a single wool blanket was not nearly enough. So the accommodations were Spartan but very, very cheap and spectacularly located and worth becoming an artist of some kind purely in hopes of spending a few months there. From my tiny balcony I could survey the street below and, off to the right, watch the Seine flowing beside the Île Saint-Louis's limestone embankment. In the distance, the blocky Tour Montparnasse stuck up like an unwhacked mole.

(Here's a Paris joke. Q: Why is the best view in Paris from the Tour Montparnasse? A: Because it's the only place where you can't see the Tour Montparnasse.)

Residents of the Cité are supposed to speak French to one another. Ideally. I had taken a year of French in college, but the only phrases that stuck with me were the ones that related specifically to our textbook's ongoing plotline about corporate espionage (*espionnage industriel*). I didn't know how to order food in a restaurant, but I knew how to demand the whereabouts of the files (*Où sont les fichiers?*) and break the news that the body is in the canal (*Le corps est dans le canal*) and casually observe that somebody has a knife in his back (*Il y a un couteau dans le dos*). I certainly didn't know how to make small talk.

The composer and I, when we'd met in the annex's ponderously slow and ominously creaky elevator, had exchanged *bonjours* and then, in English because he hadn't asked for the location of the files or the body or the knife, established that we lived across the hall from each other.

"We should have a coffee sometime," he said.

"Definitely! Anytime!" I agreed with enthusiasm that must later have struck him as needlessly disingenuous bordering on straight-up weird.

My whole life I've been both shy and social. Strangers make me anxious, but as an adult I've learned to tamp down that anxiety and talk to people anyway. Once, at a book festival that involved several cocktail parties and dinners that were absolutely crawling with strangers, I was telling another author how I enjoyed the chitchat events but also found them exhausting. I described myself as shy. He shook his head. "You're a gregarious shy person," he said. "You can do the sociable thing, but you don't draw power from it the way real extroverts do. It takes something out of you." This struck me as almost eerily true, coming from someone I'd only just met. Takes one to know one.

Which is to say that under normal circumstances I would have gone to coffee with the composer, and he and I might have become friends or at least muddled through an amiable if potentially awkward conversation. ("So, do the singers wear snorkels?") In the Hollywood version, because we were in Paris, that magnificent aphrodisiac of a city so exquisitely beautiful it tricks you into believing you are owed an equally picturesque life, coffee would have turned into a long afternoon of conversation followed a chilly walk along the Seine as the streetlamps winked on, which would have segued into a soft-focus montage of a cozy winter romance: scenic walks in overcoats and chicly knotted scarves though the Bois du Boulogne, artistic toiling in our studios, leisurely meals at Left Bank bistros, copious wine, copious leisurely soft-focus sex. Everyone knows that's what you're supposed to do in Paris, or that's what Paris is supposed to do for you. But once I was out of the elevator and back in my safe little hidey-hole *atelier* with my hot plate and my bare white walls and insufficient bedding, the idea of voluntarily having a conversation with a stranger seemed impossibly difficult, downright frightening, and generally out of the question. Being alone is simple. Other people are unpredictable; they complicate things.

So I didn't answer the phone or my neighbor's knock. For weeks, I went so far as to listen at the door before I left my studio and peer underneath, checking to make sure the hall light timer had switched off so I would be less likely to run into anyone on my way to the elevator.

I first discovered my tolerance—my affinity—for solitude in 2008. I had finished my master's degree at the University of Iowa and, thanks to a small fellowship and paltry savings and occasional emergency bailouts from my parents, I was spending eight months on Nantucket (the cold months, October through May). I was trying to write a novel that was set on a Nantucket-esque island, and I thought being immersed in the setting would be helpful in getting the atmosphere and landscape right. As it turned out, being there *was* helpful, although not for the reasons I had anticipated. The atmosphere that surrounded me was nothing like the atmosphere in my book. I was writing about a vacation island in summer, full of bustle and resortwear and sunshine, when restaurants are full and beaches dotted with bright umbrellas, a place very different from the gray, windswept, semi-abandoned scrap of land where I found myself living among leafless trees and closed-up, empty houses. People do live on Nantucket in the winter, but I knew no one and didn't meet anyone. During my most isolated stretch, beyond saying thank you for my change in the grocery store, I didn't have a face-to-face conversation with another person for five weeks.

Instead, I stayed home and wrote my book. I worked in the mornings, then took my dog for a long walk in the early afternoon, then came home and had a beer and some popcorn and watched the DVDs that Netflix kindly sent over from the distant-seeming mainland. In the evening, after dinner, I went back to work or I read in the armchair my dog and I were in constant competition for, each hurrying to occupy it the moment the other vacated.

I found that having no social life can be a boon to efficiency. Noise and brain jabber dropped away. In the ensuing quiet, I found a particularly potent focus, and after seven months I had a complete draft of my novel, four hundred pages long. I had also found a way to be content living a largely internal life. Admittedly, I got a little strange during that Nantucket winter, disproportionately worried about small choices and tasks and overly bound to my daily routine, but, after the first couple of months, I found I was never bored and very seldom lonely. I became self-sufficient in a way I hadn't known it was possible for me to be.

In Paris, I was working on my second book, a novel about ballet dancers set in New York, Southern California, and—this bright idea occurred to me once I was there—Paris. I slid easily back into solitude. I established a new loner routine. Most days I would wake up and eat a simple breakfast in my studio and then pack up my computer bag and set off for one of the city's many Starbucks.

I know, I know.

That's so American of me, so *dull* and *corporate* and *safe*, to choose Starbucks in a city chockablock with charming cafés, both new hip ones and classic ones with zinc counters and bentwood chairs and white-aproned waiters. Starbucks has no place in anyone's beautiful, romantic Parisian-montage life. True. Yes. But listen, those authentically French cafés usually don't have an abundance of electrical outlets for one's laptop, nor do they universally welcome excessive lingering over coffees that come in sizes *petite* to *très petite*. Starbucks sells giant coffees, and you can move in permanently for all they care. Parisian teenagers go to Starbucks to eat pancakes (in France, weirdly, they sell pancakes at Starbucks) and to make out. Often my laptop and I would be cozied up in an armchair directly across from an identical armchair containing two intertwined French kids, the girls with long manes of that mysteriously glossy Frenchwoman hair, the boys skinny and fashionable, both maker-outers maintaining bored expressions as they industriously smooched and groped.

After I ran out of writing energy, my goal for every day was to walk somewhere I hadn't been. My new place could be just one small street or an entire neighborhood, a cemetery or a museum or a park or a store. I wanted to explore the city a little bit at a time, no hurry. The winter is a fantastic time to walk in Paris, when there are few tourists and the city is just going about its business. I walked grand boulevards and narrow alleys. As snow sifted down from low clouds, I walked along the iced-over Canal Saint-Martin on my way to an afternoon showing of *The Descendants*. I strolled under denuded branches in the Tuileries and around the big fountain in the Jardin du Luxembourg, its water frozen into a cascading ice chandelier. During the winter sales I dug through bins of marked-down lingerie at Printemps even though I had no one to wear any of it for. I took in the stately pomp of the Pantheon, admired the stained-glass jewel box that is Sainte-Chappelle, watched white clouds of my breath dissipate in Notre-Dame's majestic nave. I visited the graves of Jean-Paul Sartre and Simone de Beauvoir, Susan Sontag, Marguerite Duras, Victor Hugo, Marie Curie. I climbed to the dome of Sacré-Coeur. I peered into shadowy cast-iron family chapels decaying among the graves at Père Lachaise. I walked the bone-lined tunnels of the catacombs. (Paris seems like an okay place to be dead—good company, at least.)

I did the usual Paris tourist stuff but at an unhurried pace, guided only by my own inclinations. I looked at people, at shop windows, at buildings, at the sky and the sidewalks and the bountiful dog poop on the sidewalks. I looked at the river. Once, late at night, I watched two giant rats jumping gleefully in and out of a trash can on the Pont Marie, squeaking away. Actively looking—noticing—is a bulwark against boredom. When I'm alone, I like that there's no pressure to turn what I see into conversation, to describe or opine in the moment. Days spent alone aren't filtered through anyone else's moods or subject to another's whims or preferences; likewise, I don't have to manage or compromise my own moods or whims, because they don't affect anyone but me.

Since France is a nation of food geniuses, I did a lot of eating. Since I was alone, I ate what I wanted, when I wanted. A late breakfast of roast chicken? Sure. Tarte tatin and red wine for dinner? Why not? I explored the *boulangeries* and *patisseries* and warring falafel joints in my neighborhood, worked my way through a marzipan-filled Epiphany cake, developed a fondness for the Breton butter pastries called *kouign amann* (added bonus: the shop that sold them was self-service, meaning I didn't have to talk to anyone), walked across the river to the food hall at Le Bon Marche and marveled at the cheese and the olives and the filmy slices of prosciutto and the yogurt aisle, which is the Platonic ideal of yogurt aisles. Even the soup-in-a-box I bought at Monoprix and heated up on my studio's hot plate was more delicious than it had any right to be.

As a resident of the Cité, I had an identity card that granted me free access to most museums—through the season pass–holders' entrances, no less, where there were never lines. I could meander through one or two galleries in the Musée d'Orsay, go back another day to see a few more, go back again later. One rainy afternoon, I sat in the Musée de l'Orangerie with no one else around, a private vista of Monet's water lilies wrapped around me.

There was vastly more to do in Paris in winter than on Nantucket in winter and exponentially more people around, but in the City of Light I found myself as heavily cloaked in solitude as I had been on the Off-Season Island of Very Little Light. This was because my aloneness was the product of an internal decision, an intentional shifting of gears, not a state imposed on me by external circumstances. A sense of purpose distinguished my solitude from loneliness, even protected me from it. I had chosen to be absorbed by my work, to encounter the city on my own terms, to retreat into myself.

To this day I almost never get lonely when I am by myself,

but I am sometimes lonely among other people: at a party where I feel out of place, for example, or when I'm angry at a loved one or drained by too much small talk. Loneliness, for me, isn't rooted in the fact of being alone but in feelings of estrangement from others, in frustration and disappointment at the imperfection of my connections. Of course, all human connections are imperfect, and loneliness is part of being human. Each of us is isolated inside one consciousness, one body, one life, and so we are all inherently and permanently alone. But most of us spend our lives making endlessly hopeful attempts to connect, to peck our way out of our aloneness like chicks out of eggs, and there is a great and poignant beauty in the effort and great joy and peril in our successes. At the same time, maybe the sanctuary of the self, where you are both king and kingdom, is too often forgotten and neglected.

In France, my aloneness was intensified by my incompetence at the language. The city babbled around me, stray words catching my comprehension but none of it solidifying into any sense of what was being said. We kept private from each other, Paris and I. It was, perhaps, like listening to an underwater opera. One day, when I was out walking, a man fell into step beside me and said something. I apologized and said I didn't understand (in French, I'll have you know—I can manage that much). "Oh, you're not French," he said in English. "What are you?"

"I'm American," I said, a little sheepishly.

He took my hand. "I love Americans!" he said. For a few steps, we walked along like that, hand in hand, but said nothing else. Then he lifted my hand, kissed the back of it, and was gone.

In March, as warm days began to be interspersed with the chilly ones, my solitude began to thaw, too. My brother came to town for a couple of days, and a night out with his colleagues went rapidly off the rails until we found ourselves bedecked in glow bracelets, dancing at three A.M. in a subterranean cave (I think it was a cave, anyway). Around the same time, I made a friend, Courtney, an American writer married to a Frenchman. Another friend, Michelle, came to visit, and when I found myself out in a bar with her and Courtney, talking and drinking, I realized I was perilously close to having a social life again.

Then there was the night I missed one person in particular. I went to see the Paris Opéra Ballet dance *La Bayadère*. The Opéra Bastille, which seats more than 2,700, was packed, the audience elegantly and sparklingly dressed and serious about ballet and discerning about their intermission Champagne. Near the end of Act I, as Nikiya danced her mournful, sensual solo at her lover's wedding, the distinguished older French gentleman next to me who had been wiping away the occasional tear since the curtain rose began to tremble and quake. His shoulders jolting up and down, he pulled a handkerchief from the inside pocket of his blazer and mopped his tear-streaked face. In the half light, he gave me an apologetic shrug that seemed to ask how he could possibly *not* be undone by something so beautiful. How?

My mother had started taking me to the ballet four times a year when I was a kindergartner in Southern California, and her love of dance, which I had absorbed slowly over the years, was at the bedrock of the novel I was writing in my stark little studio and in all those corporate coffee armchairs. I thought I was all alone when I was working, but I wasn't, really. She was more than five thousand miles away but with me in Paris, too, animating the imaginary people I was writing about, shaping their world. The night outside the theater was cold; the sidewalk gleamed with frost. I called her as I walked home, clattering over slick cobblestones in heels. I told her I wished she had been there to see the performance, that she would have loved it.

At that moment, being alone felt inadequate. What I most wanted my mother to have shared with me wasn't the ballet itself—though it was marvelous—but the feeling of communal wonder among the audience, the openness with which the man beside me wept. Art is nothing if not a naked, earnest attempt to connect, to transcend aloneness, and that night, connection had lit the theater from within the way lightning flashes and flickers inside a thunderhead. I wished I could have taken a break from my aloneness to go to the ballet with my mother, so we could be bound together by the shared experience and then by its memory. I felt an irony in the fact that I seemed to need to cut myself off from other people in order to make something—a book, a story—that I hoped would resonate with readers I would never meet, bring them into the lives and minds of characters who didn't exist. I walked home over slick pavement that gleamed like an empty stage.

It would be nice to say the balmy spring days and blooming trees at the end of March drew me out of myself enough to knock on the Swiss composer's door to offer my apologies and invite him for coffee. But the last time I saw him was when we passed each other on the Cold War–chic staircase in the annex. I'd chosen the stairs because someone had been waiting for the elevator when I came in, and I'd learned my lesson about sharing elevators with people. I was going up, and the composer was coming down. As we passed, I nodded briskly, as though I'd never seen him before, and said, "*Bonjour.*"

"*Bonjour,*" he said.

I kept climbing, but I heard that his footsteps had stopped. When I was another flight up, I stopped, too, and peered over the banister. He was looking up at me. "I am your neighbor," he called plaintively.

I regarded him in silence for a few seconds, then pulled back into the shadows and continued to climb.

⚜ ⚜ ⚜

**Maggie Shipstead** is the author of two novels: *Astonish Me* and *Seating Arrangements*, which was a *New York Times* bestseller and winner of the Dylan Thomas Prize and the *Los Angeles Times* Book Prize for First Fiction. She is a graduate of Harvard and the Iowa Writers' Workshop and a former Wallace Stegner Fellow at Stanford.

***Say bonjour:***
    maggieshipstead.com
    Facebook: /MaggieShipsteadAuthor

Instagram: @Shipstead
Twitter: @MaggieShipstead

**The Paris Book:**
*Astonish Me*

**Favorite Paris moment:**

Watching from my balcony late one night as snow
blanketed my neighborhood's rooftops and
cobblestone alleyways—everything was so quiet. No
one was around. Truly quiet moments in big, busy
cities have a sacred feeling to them.

**Least favorite Paris moment:**

Getting nervous every time I needed to buy
something because my French is so bad. This was
nobody's fault but mine. Thankfully, most Parisians
have better English than I do French and are really
nice about speaking it these days.

**Favorite quote about Paris:**

"In Paris, everybody wants to be an actor; nobody is
content to be a spectator."—Jean Cocteau

**Song that reminds you of Paris:**

"*Quelqu'un m'a dit*" by Carla Bruni. I listened to that
song a lot during my winter in Paris—the stripped-
down, bittersweet sound seemed just right for gray
weather and leafless trees. Bruni, who's almost painfully
chic and talented, was First Lady of France at the time.

**In Paris, you can skip . . .**

I spent a lot of time at Starbucks, so maybe this
makes me a hypocrite, but don't eat at tourist trap
restaurants with laminated menus in English. You
can do better, and you might as well take advantage
of being in a nation of food geniuses.

**In Paris, you must . . .**

Visit the catacombs. Paris has a sprawling
underworld of tunnels, most of which are off-limits,
but the section of the catacombs open to tourists
provides at least a peek at the city beneath the city
and is also a powerful reminder of the centuries of
Parisians who came before.

⚜ ⚜ ⚜

# THIRTY-FOUR THINGS YOU SHOULD KNOW ABOUT PARIS

*Meg Waite Clayton*

The intended ending to the honeymoon was Paris. Years before—before I'd ever seen anything of Paris beyond the postcards passed around in my French language classes—a lawyer friend of mine was going there routinely for work. I wanted his job, of course. Who wouldn't? But he assured me the only difference between a conference room in Paris and one in New York is the length of a commute.

So the first thing anyone planning to visit Paris should know is that conference rooms are to be avoided at all costs. To be honest, the same is true of New York.

By the time of our honeymoon-planning, though—largely done by a travel agent I never met, as I was a full-fledged lawyer myself by then, closing three corporate deals in the week before I toddled down the aisle—it was my Charming Companion-in-Life-to-Be (hereinafter "C.C.") who wanted to end our honeymoon in Paris.

I'd visited Paris three years earlier, an experience I wasn't eager to repeat. I didn't remember seeing the Eiffel Tower or the Louvre, although certainly I must have. I remember exactly two things from that first trip: Monet's Water Lilies, and the last wracking gasps of a relationship in some crappy little hotel room. (I should warn you, all hotel rooms in Paris are small.) I recommend avoiding trips to Paris with lovers who are soon to be ex-lovers. Even Paris can only take so much.

For that matter, you might want to eschew lawyer- and business-type traveling companions in favor of artists painting at easels beside the Seine, or writers pouring words into journals while you sip a good Burgundy with them. If you happen to have the misfortune of being a lawyer or business type yourself, or in love with one, or both (as I was), don a mustache and dark glasses, a beret, one of those gorgeous French scarves.

So having had one two-lawyer relationship tank in Paris, I wasn't keen on ending my two-lawyer honeymoon there. But, being even less keen to explain to C.C. exactly why I wasn't keen, I said Paris, sure, Paris. Why not?

In the end, we came to the city almost directly from a place in the Italian Lake District we loved so much that we gave them all our money, cancelled our plans for the south of France, and rearranged everything so that we spent as much time as possible on Lake Como—conveniently leaving only two nights and a day in Paris. Thirty-six hours in Paris. What could go wrong?

We arrived late, and checked into our small but extravagantly expensive hotel room, and we slept in late and stayed in our pajamas while we ate the small but expensive croissants we'd had brought up to our room. Yes, there was some honeymoon-type activity, too, if you must know. It was the last day of our trip, and C.C.'s birthday as well. But finally, we pulled on our walking shoes and went down to the hotel lobby—which was, now that I think of it, shockingly empty, everyone else apparently quite aware that there was something more important to do at this particular moment of this particular day than what we were doing, which was asking the concierge if he might reserve us a table for dinner that night at Tour d'Argent.

"This is the finest restaurant in all of Paris," the concierge assured us in impeccable English.

"Yes, we'd love a window table if possible," C.C. said. C.C., in case I haven't mentioned it, is from the South, so do imagine that line in a warm but subtle Southern accent of the type Southerners who've been away from the South for years often still have.

"It will not be possible," the concierge assured us. "This restaurant, it must be booked six months in advance, even on a day that is not today."

If we'd been paying attention, we might have been puzzled by his mentioning "a day that is not today," and the empty lobby, and the way the poor concierge kept glancing longingly at the door. But no. C.C. set to getting his way (which he rarely fails to do), jawboning the poor fellow in his charming Southern way. He played the honeymoon card, indicating his "beautiful bride" (which, yes, did score points with me, if not with the concierge), and the birthday card, and the last-night-in-Paris card. Before you could say, "You American fools, don't you know what you're making me miss?" the concierge was phoning the restaurant and finding us a cancellation, and a reservation at whatever ungodly late hour they started serving. The sun doesn't set until eleven P.M. in Paris in the summer, and what kind of romantic dinner starts before dark? You do need to know this about Paris. Sometimes, it seems the sun never will set.

The sidewalks of the Champs-Élysées, when we finally stepped out from the hotel lobby, were surprisingly crowded, everyone lined up along the empty street like Germans waiting for a crossing light to change. We joined the throng, improbably watching the empty street ourselves.

"What's going on?" my new husband asked, not in French.

There followed a flurry of conversation—in a rapid French for which my high school classes did not prepare me. I did catch "*les idiots américains.*"

"*S'il vous plait, vous parlez plus lentement?*" I said, digging the words to request that they speak more slowly from the bit of my brain that had grown even rustier in the years since that first fateful Paris adventure.

Someone did finally speak to us slowly enough that I could pick out "*bicyclettes.*"

"*Les bicyclettes?*" I said. Bicycles?

Most of the French around us—perhaps all of them—made that *pffffffit* sound with their lips that is so dismissively French.

Not a minute later, bicyclers sped past and the crowd went *très fou*, waving and cheering. We'd stumbled onto the finish of the Tour de France. The seventy-fifth Tour de France, no less. Twenty-one days and twenty-two hundred miles of a race that had actually, unbeknownst to us, started on our wedding day. A fellow from Spain was given the yellow jersey. We didn't stay for that, as we had only the one day in Paris, and we wanted to walk through the Jardin des Tuileries and along the Seine.

It rains in Paris, by the way. *Il pleut* almost half the days of the year. It's not something you imagine, when you imagine Paris. You imagine the Mona Lisa, although perhaps not the crowd around it, perhaps not the bulletproof glass. You imagine Notre-Dame, which, if you're lucky, you will see by candlelight, with a surprisingly small number of monks filling the voluminous cathedral with Gregorian chants. You imagine the Eiffel Tower, tickets for which, you may want to know, can be bought in advance and yes, you do want the just-before-sunset elevator, trust me on this. (This is more difficult than you might imagine, as the French, being French, don't actually put the tickets on sale on any identifiable schedule. Plan ahead, check the website often, bang your head against the wall when, despite your best efforts, the tickets you want mysteriously disappear as you are reloading the dang page.)

It rained that last night of our honeymoon, but not until we were well into a bottle of wine at the Tour d'Argent—we'd meant to order white, but what came was red and we were quite sure the mistake was ours. The view of raindrops on the Seine was lovely, actually. We had no umbrella, though, so rather than walking along the river in the rain, we took a cab back and . . . well, as I said, it was the last night of our honeymoon.

It seems random and improbable that every time I find myself in Paris, something remarkable is going on, but the thing is, it's Paris. You really should know that if you walk in Paris, you'll see some gorgeous thing at every turn. We've stumbled onto an extraordinary quartet practicing in a church, a cellist playing in one archway into the Louvre where the acoustics are fantastic, assorted political rallies and fashion shoots, and once, a George Clooney filming. Well, I was pretty sure it was Clooney, and C.C. is wise enough to go along with my story.

The French are awfully enthusiastic at celebrating en masse, so if something *big* is going on you'll likely find out eventually. The third time I was there, they won the World Cup, or perhaps it was the game to get them into the finals of the World Cup, but in any event the party in the streets went all night. During my fourth visit, Hollande was elected president, and we followed gobs of Parisians waving flags as they streamed down the street, headed for, it turned out (we had no idea, but we followed them anyway), the Bastille. The Bastille, you should know, doesn't look like much now—just a random big traffic circle with a monument in the middle that would be something in any other city, but is slightly pedestrian when your choices include Sacré-Coeur, Notre-Dame, l'Hôtel de Ville and la Tour Eiffel, Sainte-Chapelle, l'Opera, l'Arc de Triomphe, and the Louvre, which was a thing of beauty even before its glass pyramid was added to light up the night. (Do, by the way, see that pyramid at night.) But a prison stood in this area until, in the opening days of the French Revolution (1789, I've looked it up so you don't have to), an armed mob stormed the prison gates, and the place remains today one of the most popular gathering spots for the French to celebrate or protest, which they appear to enjoy in equal measure. It was quite a party to celebrate Hollande's victory, and we might have stayed all night except that I'm not that tall and the square was so crowded that C.C. began to worry (and I did, too) that I would be suffocated or trampled, the first casualty of a new era in France.

That trip—my fourth to Paris—was the first time C.C. and I basked in the luxury of an entire month there. It was April, and it rained every day of that trip but one. So add that to the list of things to know: despite all the singing about April in Paris (Frank Sinatra, Ella Fitzgerald, Billie Holliday, Louis Armstrong, and even Doris Day), if you have a choice, go in May. You will probably not listen to me on this. You'll be in good company; I didn't listen to my friend who tried to tell me, either. Who to believe—Sinatra, or a friend who has neither mesmerizing blue eyes nor that gorgeously persuasive voice?

The good news for you—and for C.C. and me, of course—is that the Jardin des Tuileries studded with brightly colored umbrellas is almost more gorgeous than it is in sunshine. And, like everything else there is to do in this world, Paris does umbrellas better than anyplace. Bright orange is best, one big enough to share with your lover. A Champagne house name at the edge is optional, but the Veuve Clicquot orange is *très chic*. Or C.C. and I think it is, anyway.

If it's a chilly rain—and it will be if you're there in April—slip into a café and order a *chocolat chaud*. Don't ask for marshmallows. It's not that kind of chocolate. It will come with the highest-quality chocolate melted at the bottom of the cup, and steamed whole milk, and whipped cream and a spoon. You can share it with your writer or your artist or your lawyer-incognito if you want to prove yourself more generous than I.

Oh, go ahead: When the only one looking is that adorable dog the woman at the table next to you brought, lick the bottom of the cup. Me, I'm thinking I'm being discreet when I run my finger through the last delicious little pool of melted chocolate that somehow escapes blending with the warm milk.

And the good news is that rain tends to nip in for a quick visit to Paris, a few minutes or perhaps an hour, rarely with plans for a longer stay. By the time your cup is licked, the clouds will likely have moved on to some dryer bit of France, leaving you to explore a slightly dampened but still delightful place, at least until the clouds return the next day.

And somehow, it almost never rains at sunset, which as I said comes quite late. For sunset, you have a few choices, the first being the tickets to the Eiffel Tower I hope you have in your hands. If you can afford it, buy tickets for two different nights, just in case it does rain, even though it probably won't. You will not regret going up a second time. And do look down when you get to the top, but be ready for it. It's far more terrifying that you imagine it will be. Also far more beautiful.

So you've done the Eiffel Tower or have your tickets for another night, or you've decided not to go up for some unfathomable reason, and you're interested in the more traditional Sunset Option behind Curtain Number 2? This tends to involve expensive restaurants and three-hour meals, generally with no view whatsoever of the sunset or anything else, and tables cozied up to one another in a way that is not the least bit cozy. I confess to having very little experience in this alternative; that Tour d'Argent evening on our honeymoon . . . well, it *was* our honeymoon, and unlike most Paris restaurants it did at least have a view, and I was a lawyer-incognito and C.C. was a highly overpaid lawyer-incognito, and we could afford more money than time.

We traded in the big lawyer paychecks for considerably smaller writing ones, but the upside is we're writers-with-our-journals-on-the-Seine, no incognito about it. It makes me laugh every time I say that, like I've just won the best-life lottery. As writers, we don't ever actually have to go home except on account of our dog, much less keep track of every working minute of our lives in six-minute increments to be billed out at the cost of one of those Paris dinners. The only downside is the paying-for-our-adventures part.

Which is one of the many beauties of the Sunset Option behind Door Number 3—which is the way C.C. and I spend nearly every evening in Paris. And we never tire of it.

This kind of evening involves a bit of good eats you can buy at just about any little market in town for $10, a bottle of Languedoc or Vouvray or Muscadet you can get for even less, and a bench with a view. C.C. and I prefer the Rive Gauche—the left bank—where there is an absolutely charming little wine shop, La Dernière Goutte, on rue de Bourbon le Château. They often host free tastings, and your sin of knowing nothing at all about French wines before you arrive will never gain you the charge of being "*les idiots américains*" or even a single *pfffffftt*.

Our three-block sunset-picnic-stocking route begins at the

wine shop, where you ought to just take their advice. From there, we cross the street to Henri Le Roux Chocolatier et Caramélier, where chocolate comes in so many varieties—all described in French—that you might be overwhelmed. I suggest a single bar of Embruns, which sounds unappetizing, I know, this is one of the very few things in the world that sounds better in English: "sea spray." We're talking 67 percent dark chocolate with *fleur de sel de Guérande*, which is fine Breton sea salt. You might think that's all you need, wine and chocolate, and sometimes it is. But there is conveniently a little roasted chicken rotisserie and a fruit and vegetable stand on rue de Buci, at the end of the block. There are also adorable little places where you can get great pâté (for this, I'm afraid I leave you in C.C.'s hands; I hate pâté), and cheese, and thin little ham slices, and salads. It's a single all-you-need block, except for the bread.

Just so you know, even if you're used to swanky U.S.-bakery bread, you have not eaten bread until you've eaten Parisian bakery bread. At the risk of wading into the best-Paris-bakery squabbles, I'm going to tell you that you can just carry on down rue de Buci to a little street called either rue Mazarine or rue de l'Ancienne Comédie, depending on which way you look. Yes, this is a little Parisian joke on the rest of us, this constant changing of street names. Look to the right (the funny direction, that comedy street), and you'll see Eric Kayser Boulanger.

You might think you could do the route in the other direction, starting with the *boulanger*, and C.C. and I have tried that at time or two. But here's the thing: *boulanger* translates to something like, "To hell with that low-carb nonsense, what is life without bread?" You want to get your baguette last, as you will not be able to keep from breaking the end off while it is still warm. It really is most delicious in bites snuck from the bag. But I'm very sorry to tell you that if you carry the bread for the time it takes to collect the chicken and wine and chocolate, you will be left with no bread for your dinner.

Yes, you must choose the plain white-flour baguette. I know, your nutritionist would be appalled. My advice is to think about how many baguettes you can get for whatever you pay that nutritionist, and ask yourself where the better bargain is.

Me, I'm generally happy to trade all the bread for all the chocolate—which we now know is heart-healthy!—and C.C. would trade all the chocolate for the bread. But in Paris, it's pretty close.

Now the question is where to take all these goodies, and the answer is one of Paris's beautifully ubiquitous benches. If you turn right out of the bakery, you will end up in the Jardin du Luxembourg, where you can watch chess players and stroll the gorgeously manicured grounds. C.C. and I prefer the little chairs up the steps from the fountain (trust me, you'll understand what I mean when you get there, but it's hard to explain), where it is quieter and yet with a nice view back to the fountain and the château and all the people-watching anyone could want. Often, music will float out from the bandstand tucked in the woods. Romantic, right? There are many quiet places to canoodle in this park too, if you're into that kind of thing. C.C. and I admit to nothing in that regard.

Even better, rather than turning right out of the *boulanger*, turn left. In a very few minutes, you will come out on the Seine, just a few feet from the Pont des Artes.

You might know the Pont des Artes as "the bridge formerly known as the love locks bridge." If you don't know what this means, imagine you and your lawyer-incognito come to this bridge, buy a lock from a hawker there, lock it to the bridge, and, in a gesture of eternal love, throw the key into the water. It sounds quite romantic until you see locks crawling like kudzu all over the bridge, threatening not only its beauty but also its structural integrity on account of the weight of a million locks. (Never mind the environmental damage of a million keys in the Seine.) Also, I'm just going to say I wouldn't put too much stock in an eternal gesture that can be repeated with another lover the next afternoon for a mere euro or two.

So the Pont des Arts is a walking bridge—traffic-free—that crosses from the left bank to the Louvre and the Jardin des Tuileries. Both the Louvre and the garden are fine places to picnic, and to canoodle if, again, you and your lawyer-in-disguise are into that. But here's the thing: On the Pont des Arts itself, there is always some young clarinet-or-guitar-or-cello-playing kid who belongs at Carnegie Hall. It has nice benches, but you might rather sit on the wooden bridge itself, leaning against the lock-free bridge. Yes, the isles do look beautiful in evening light, but sit with your back to them, because the sun sets in the other direction. The Seine looks spectacular from the bridge at sunset, and, as a bonus prize, the Eiffel Tower will light up just for you and your lawyer-incognito, giving you the world's best view of this remarkable monument sparkling to life.

I should perhaps mention here that Parisians smoke more than you might like if you're not a smoker. (Me, I'm not a smoker, and C.C. is the worst kind of nonsmoker, which is the kind who used to smoke and had a hell of a time giving it up.) But if some passerby accidentally flicks his ashes at you as you're enjoying your wine (you did bring a corkscrew and glasses, didn't you?), just remind yourself that these Parisians are of the same stock as those who, when they learned Hitler meant to visit that Eiffel Tower in front of you, cut the cable to the elevator rather than letting him go up. Also, they make that wine you're drinking, and the chocolate and the bread. Veuve Clicquot. Chanel. Givenchy. Cartier. Hermès (the scarves) or Hermé (the chocolate). What's a Gauloises or a Gitane every now and then compared to all that?

Do wave at the tourists passing by on the boats, though, and take their pictures. It makes them inordinately happy as they are paying $20 per drink in addition to their ticket cost to look up at you, while you and your own C.C. are enjoying the evening for the cost of those $10 worth of irresistible eats and that one bottle of wine.

I'd like to say that C.C. and I thought of bringing the wine to the bridge ourselves, but it's possible that the first wine we ever drank there came from the bottle of a very nice couple visiting from the Midwest, where everyone shares everything. We politely declined at first, and then we thought, *Why not?* It was such a nice gesture that we like to pay it forward. So if a middle-aged blond woman and her husband with the Southern accent offer you a glass of wine on the bridge, do simply say "*merci*" and raise a glass to new friends in a rumbling old city that, like the best of loves, grows more enchanting with time.

⚜ ⚜ ⚜

**Meg Waite Clayton** is the *New York Times* and *USA Today* bestselling author of five novels, most recently the Langum Prize–honored national bestseller *The Race for Paris*. Meg's previous novels include *The Wednesday Sisters*, one of *Entertainment Weekly's* 25 Essential Best Friend Novels of all time, and *The Language of Light*, a finalist for the Bellwether Prize (now the PEN/Bellwether). Meg's shorter works include more than fifty pieces which have appeared in, among others, the *Los Angeles Times*, *The New York Times*, *The Washington Post*, the *San Francisco Chronicle*, *Runner's World*, and *The Literary Review*, and on public radio.

### *Say bonjour:*

megwaiteclayton.com
Facebook: /NovelistMeg
Instagram: @MegWaiteClayton
Twitter: @MegWClayton

### *The Paris Book:*

*The Race for Paris*

### *Favorite book about Paris:*

*Hunting and Gathering* by Anna Gavalda. Written by a Paris-born author, it is a quirky, absolutely charming insider's look at Paris through the lives of four occupants of a Paris apartment house: a struggling young artist who works as an office cleaner at night, a young aristocrat misfit, a cook, and an elderly grandmother.

**Favorite non-Paris travel destination:**

China in 1984, shortly after it had opened to Americans, remains the most fascinating place I have ever been. It was like stepping back in time, and in such a different culture, before it was overrun with tourism and smog. American travelers were still rare enough that little schoolgirls even in Shanghai followed and spied on my six-foot-four traveling companion and shorter, blonder me. I returned twenty years later to a completely different China.

**In Paris, you can skip . . .**

Perhaps this is sacrilegious—and I can't say I've done anything I wouldn't do again in Paris—but I eschew hotels (small, expensive rooms) and restaurants (expensive, if not small, plates) for apartments and picnics on the Seine.

**In Paris, you must . . .**

My essay mentions a few, but you could spend a lifetime in Paris . . . Do try the chocolate—all the different shops so you can be sure which is best! Climb the Eiffel Tower for sunset. The Louvre courtyard late night, lit up and quiet. The Manet portrait of Berthe Morisot at the Musée d'Orsay. Writing in the Jardin des Tuileries. The *chocolat chaud,* which is a different thing entirely from American hot chocolate.

✤ ✤ ✤

# THANKS TO . . .

Elizabeth Winick Rubinstein, for believing in this project and providing transatlantic therapy sessions.

Chris Pepe, for your energy and enthusiasm, and always being willing to talk about Paris.

The team at Putnam Books, for all your support and hard work, especially Ivan Held, Karen Fink, Carolyn Darr, Anabel Pasarow, Ashley McClay, and Emily Ollis.

Monica Cordova, Ploy Siripant, and David Cherrytree for the beautiful cover.

Hanne Blank, Meghan Daum, and Victoria Zackheim for generously sharing your editorial wisdom and experience.

Every one of the contributors to this anthology, for bringing your voices and giving us the chance to experience Paris in new ways. Special thanks to Paula McLain, whose essay inspired the title of this anthology.

## THANKS TO . . .

The statue of Georges Danton at the Odéon Métro station, for making me feel like a champion every time I came up the escalator.

Chris, for being the best traveling companion, and for always being willing to ask, "Do you speak English?"

Paris, for offering us so many stories, and you, for reading them.